THE TIGER AND THE ROSE

VERNON SCANNELL

The Tiger
and the
Rose

AN AUTOBIOGRAPHY

HAMISH HAMILTON
LONDON

First published in Great Britain, 1971
by Hamish Hamilton Ltd
90 Great Russell Street, London WC1

Copyright © 1971 by Vernon Scannell

SBN 241 02054 9

Printed in Great Britain
by Ebenezer Baylis & Son Ltd
The Trinity Press, Worcester, and London

In me, past, present, future meet
To hold long chiding conference.
My lusts usurp the present tense
And strangle Reason in his seat.
My loves leap through the future's fence
To dance with dream-enfranchised feet.

In me the cave-man clasps the seer,
And garlanded Apollo goes
Chanting to Abraham's deaf ear.
In me the tiger sniffs the rose.
   Look in my heart, kind friends, and tremble,
   Since there your elements assemble.

Selected Poems—SIEGFRIED SASSOON

NOW

IT IS January and the sky above Payne's Hill is sour and grimed. Soon darkness will have fallen and the children will at last get to bed, the boys first because the girls are older and have serious homework to do, and I shall read to Toby and John for ten minutes or so, and then come back to my room and maybe write a bit more or, far more likely, bumble among old letters and abortive verses, make vague dishonest plans for a future of systematic industry, and then walk down to The Griffin's Head for a couple of pints of farm cider and maybe a draught Guinness or two to finish up on. It is not a bad life.

This part of Dorset is a good place to live. The village people are friendly and the countryside is much as it was a hundred years ago. We like it here. We are, I suppose, as contented as it would be reasonable to expect. I ought to be grateful. I am grateful. And yet. It is January, the month of my birth, and I am forty-eight. The road ahead gets shorter and less inviting: the sense of expectancy that one used to wake up with, the excitement of not knowing quite what the day was holding in its unopened fist, is something that will never come again. Perhaps it is just as well. I have had my share of excitement and extremes of experience, boredom, misery, delight, terror, rage, longing and desire. I use the first person singular, the autobiographical 'I', but the 'I' that endured or enjoyed past experience is not the same 'I' that is writing these words. Yet it would be wrong to use the third person 'he'. The 'I' of, say, twenty-five years ago would be astonished to see this present version of himself. Almost certainly neither would like the other and each would embarrass the other. But the past young self or selves cannot be erased any more than can the events in which they were involved. They are not dead but constantly making their claims on the present, modifying it even as they themselves are modified in the maw of subsequent events and in the memory which is part of the shaping imagination. Incidents, actions and motives lose their sharpness of outline: even the larger events, the big key occurrences are sometimes difficult to get into focus. That is why I shall try to fix them now, before they are distorted out of all resemblance to their original shapes.

Twenty-five years ago, 1945, the year that the war against Germany and Japan ended, was the year I made what might seem like a desperate decision and performed what might appear to be—depending on your values and point of view—an act of criminal folly, manic selfishness, zany recklessness, abject cowardice or even, perhaps, eccentric courage. I deserted from the Army.

THEN

I JOINED the Army at the end of 1940 when I was eighteen years old. I had tried to get into the RAF but had been turned down because of one defective eye and, romantically and foolishly, I scorned a job on the ground. The Army did not really attract me but it seemed less inglorious than a non-combatant role in the Air Force so I enlisted in the Argyll and Sutherland Highlanders, who seemed rather more glamorous than an English county regiment, and I suffered nearly two years of boredom, discomfort and misery, relieved by occasional booze-ups, some barmy hilarity and a few wild privilege leaves, before I was transferred to the Gordon Highlanders and shipped off to the Middle East. A couple of years later I was back in England, slightly bomb-happy, and waiting with fearful resignation for the invasion of Normandy. Three weeks after the landing I was wounded on patrol near Caen and brought back to a Military Hospital near Warrington where I spent about eight months before being sent to a Convalescent Depot in Hamilton, and I was there when the Germans surrendered in May 1945.

Now, I disliked the Army very much. I found that nothing in my temperament fitted me for the part of soldier. I was unpractical, any kind of mechanical apparatus threw me into a panic; I was slow at such jobs as putting equipment together, even at dressing myself, and I was usually late on parade. When I tried to do quite simple tasks like cleaning a rifle, polishing a bayonet-scabbard, blancoing webbing, I took twice as long as anyone else and usually with botched results and punitive consequences. Even my battle-dress did not fit me. I was fairly tall but, at that time, quite lean, so that trousers of suitable length were far too slack at the waist and the seat hung low and baggy like a Muslim's pantaloons. When I wore battle-order my small pack, which was supposed to sit high between

3

the shoulder blades, would sag miserably nearer the small of my back, 'like a bloody parachute', as one disgusted sergeant remarked. My companions were for the most part lively if unpredictable company in the wet canteen or local pub. I formed some friendships which were fine for the time and place but under different circumstances would never have been cemented because the needs they satisfied would not have existed. It could be argued that service in the ranks is a valuable educative experience because men of quite different types, from widely varying social environments, are forced into close relationships and compelled to establish workable bases for them, but the truth is that one or other is generally called on to make considerable sacrifice of integrity and, at the risk of sounding priggish, I would say that it is usually the more sensitive, imaginative and intelligent who has to pay the most. A more mature man than myself might have been able to retain wholeness of personality, something of his dignity and sense of his own identity, though it is questionable how successfully he would have been absorbed into his group. I was decidedly not mature. I deliberately suppressed that part of myself that I most valued. I became ashamed of my interest in literature, ideas and the arts. I consciously adopted a mask with forehead villainous low. I was already, at eighteen, greedily addicted to beer, so no acting ability was needed to play the part of boozer. My interest in boxing was genuine and my skill was respected, so it was not difficult for me to flex my muscles and roar with the roaring boys. But it was not good for me either. It was shameful and brutalizing. I did not read anything except an occasional thriller or newspaper and, although I was sometimes surprised by a sudden craving for music other than Vera Lynn or the NAAFI piano, I did not go to a concert for nearly five years.

In the summer of 1944 when I was brought back from Normandy to lie for months in hospital with both legs encased in plaster I found my starved interest in literature suddenly clamouring for nourishment. I began again to read and I realized sharply and bitterly that I had wasted five years of my life. Intellectually I was, at twenty-two, a blundering, scarcely literate eighteen-year-old.

Hospital life was utterly different from what I had become accustomed to, its circumstances so much closer to those of the civilian world I had almost forgotten. I lay in a proper bed with clean sheets. I ate and drank from china and there were nurses, women, to gentle the harsh climate of masculinity. Each bed was an island. There was no need for close relationships with the other men. One had time for thought, for observation and for reading. I read, without direction, anything I could get hold of, and the more I read the more I realized the depth and magnitude of my ignorance. The long-dormant ambition to write, which I had known since childhood, awoke strong and importunate, but I knew miserably that I was simply not equipped for the job and any small chance I had of learning the trade would be withheld while I was still in the Army.

The hospital interlude came to an end and I was posted to the old Cameronian Barracks at Hamilton, which had been taken over as a Convalescent Depot, where we spent a lot of time in the gymnasium performing remedial exercises to restore mobility to stiffened joints and limbs. Hospital blues were discarded and we were back in ordinary battle-dress. Life was undemanding compared with the strenuously boring routine of depot or camp but it was again exclusively masculine, drab, sweaty, obscene and monotonous.

We lived in large rooms in the penitential stone barracks, sleeping in two-tiered bunks over which there was much rivalry to occupy the upper berths since sleepers in the lower were in danger of being pissed on by incontinent revellers on pay-nights. In the room I was allotted there was only one man who seemed as if he might offer something other than talk of booze and bints. He spent a lot of time lying on his bunk reading a book, but when I got talking to him I found that he was the kind of barrack-room intellectual that anyone who has served in the ranks or on the lower deck will recognize: the earnest, humourless, self-regarding bore, who, since he is technically literate and may voluntarily have read a few books, considers himself not only intellectually superior to the herd, but morally and probably genetically superior as well.

He was a fussily neat man who had his battle-dress altered by a tailor so that he looked better dressed than most of us. He did not drink or smoke or swear. In civilian life, he told me, he had been 'a gentleman's gentleman'. Apart from the novels of Charles Morgan and A. J. Cronin, who were the only imaginative writers he

5

considered worth looking at, he read nothing but the most popular kind of predigested philosophy and psychology. Not that my own range of reading was any more impressive, but it was entirely different. I had read a good deal of fiction, but without discrimination, swallowing Hemingway and Jack London, Forster and Hugh Walpole, Virginia Woolf and Ethel Mannin with the same uncritical relish. It was much the same with poetry. I actually owned only one book of verse and that was the Methuen *Anthology of Modern Verse* originally published in 1921 and well-stocked with Georgian jelly babies; but it had a good selection of Hardy, some not very well-chosen Sassoon, poems by Charlotte Mew whose work still gives me pleasure though I am not now sure of how much my enjoyment comes from a nostalgic recapturing of the first excitement she gave me. There was a good deal of early Yeats and de la Mare and four poems of Wilfred Owen, including *Greater Love*, the sentimentality of which I did not care for then and care a lot less for now. At that time I had read only a very little of Auden and MacNeice and was unaware of the existence of poets of my own generation such as Alun Lewis, Sidney Keyes and Keith Douglas. Undoubtedly I was a literary ignoramus but at least I did enjoy what I read, unlike the Gentleman's Gentleman who would wade through his *Great Thinkers of the East* with no apparent pleasure, like a man grimly performing his calisthenics, convinced that the more painful the exercise the more beneficial it must be.

So in Hamilton I reverted to booze and the wistful fantasies of bints, fantasies because the reality was unlikely to be realized in that blacked-out sooty town of fish-and-chip shops and bars which were patronized only by men, places where you bought your drinks and drank them and did not waste time on chatter or anything else that would slow down the rate of consumption. I expect there may have been a dance-hall were you could pick up a girl, but I had never learnt how to dance and I pretended to despise the accomplishment; but secretly I envied it. The only proposition that came my way in Hamilton was from a woman who had both a husband and a son serving in the Army abroad. It happened like this: occasionally local families would write to the Officer Commanding the depot and offer to give hospitality to a specified number of soldiers, and these invitations were printed on the notice-board and the first men to apply would be accepted. My main companion at the time was a large Aberdonian called Douglas Alexander, a good drinker and useful ally in a brawl. Neither he nor I had taken advantage of the civilian offers of entertainment, feeling that tea and baps and community singing at the piano were not in our line, but one week we were both of us broke and had sold every article of kit that was marketable and could find no one to lend us the price of a pint. So, rather than face an evening in the barracks or prowling the dismal streets of the town, we went to the orderly-room and put down our names for an evening's hospitality at a house not far from the depot.

When Douglas and I arrived at the place, feeling rather foolish and apprehensive, the door was opened by a middle-aged woman, or what seemed to me at that time middle-aged, if not positively old. She might not have been more than forty but she had that look of firmly set solidity that the young associate with older aunts. She interrupted our mumbled attempts to introduce ourselves with an enthusiastic invitation to come in and make ourselves at home, and we were shown into the front parlour where another woman of about the same age was sitting drinking stout. On the table were plates of sandwiches, scones and cakes, and on the sideboard at least a dozen pint bottles of beer and some of those stocky little bottles of strong ale that the Scots call 'dumps' or 'wee heavies'. We began to feel more cheerful.

The second lady, a friend of our hostess, was more angular, tougher looking. She told us that her husband was in the Military Police and stationed in Italy. She looked as if she would make a pretty formidable red-cap herself. Douglas and I were encouraged to eat and drink and the first hour or so passed pleasantly enough with commonplace chat about our homes, our civilian jobs and what we intended to do when we got out of the Army. But soon after we had finished eating the ladies decided to get down to business. The lights were switched off and Douglas and I found ourselves each with a substantial woman on his lap. Mine was the hostess.

Her approach was direct and, adopted by someone twenty years younger, it might have been exciting. I was startled and embarrassed

7

but I felt her hospitality deserved some sort of repayment so I tried, without enthusiasm, to respond, but my hand encountered what felt like corrugated iron corsets and capacious slippery bloomers and these, with the hot smell of tobacco-smoke and beer that she was breathing into my face, were too much for me. I started to say something about wanting a pee but was interrupted by a roar from Douglas: 'Get away you dirty old whore.' There was a loud thump and a cry from his partner as she evidently hit the floor. I took courage from his example and heaved our hostess from my lap and got to my feet. There was a crash as Douglas blundered into the table. Then he found the light-switch and the room was lit again. Both women began to yell invective as we grabbed our greatcoats and glengarries and beat it out of the house.

When we got back to the barracks we told the Gentleman's Gentleman that we had had a wonderful evening of good food and drink and intelligent and witty conversation with two charming ladies who were very interested in cultural matters. Generously we gave him the address. I never knew whether he visited the place because a few days later the Germans surrendered and V.E. Day was celebrated. As far as I was concerned, the war was over. The Far East was not my concern and in any case the Japs would soon be beaten. I packed my shaving gear and toothbrush into a haversack and left the depot just after tea. The following evening I was dropped by a civilian lorry-driver in Cricklewood. I was on the run.

NOW

THAT was a quarter of a century ago. I now say that I deserted because I knew that if I stayed in the Army any longer I would be finished, I would become a brown automaton, a thing without imagination, intelligence, ambition. I knew that my one hope was to get out, to live as a free man, to begin to educate myself. Yet today I am almost certainly rationalizing what was done on impulse. My flight was unpremeditated, or so it seemed. But it also seemed inevitable, pre-ordained, so the decision to desert must have been forming slowly at some hidden level of consciousness. To talk of such an act in terms of courage and cowardice is, I think, meaningless, but that is not to say that it could not be condemned as totally selfish. I knew that I would be making appeals for help to people on whom I would become a burden. I did not care that close relations would be embarrassed by visits from the police. I was concerned only with my own possible salvation.

I wonder if I have changed much since then, whether now, if the circumstances of my life were to become as difficult to tolerate as they were then, I would walk out and leave my family, abandon all responsibility for them. I cannot really say, for I am bound to them by bonds of love, and without them I am diminished. I do not mean that the frettings and anxieties of domesticity, those times of airless claustrophobia, do not become onerous, nor do I mean that I am stronger and have developed a firm sense of duty; only that I am older and, perhaps, just a little wiser, wise enough to know what ought to have been obvious much earlier: that there is no escape from what one is.

I ask myself the question that every author who ventures into the booby-trapped territories of autobiographical writing must put to himself: why do it at all? W. H. Auden has said somewhere that no poet should write his autobiography because he is using up capital and, in principle, I agree with him. Most poets and, for that matter, novelists, are drawing on the material of autobiography in their imaginative works. You can find out far more about a writer from his poems or fiction than from writing which is self-avowedly auto-biographical because, in his stories or poems, his preoccupations, obsessions, moral standards, the quality of his intelligence, his loves, hates, aspirations, beliefs and fears—all that constitutes the man's individuality—insist on expression. The poet, absorbed in the solving of formal problems, the struggle with slippery eels of language, has no time for dissimulation and he tells us more about himself than he knows. The man whose conscious purpose it is to describe himself is bound to conceal or modify what is deeply shameful and present to his reader something other than the truth about himself, and if he remarks with a show of candour on his own weaknesses we are unlikely to be convinced. To say of yourself that you are vain, cruel, selfish and intolerant implies that you are also remarkably honest in admitting these faults.

Yet, believing all this, I still wish to recapture what I can of those parts of the past that seem to have been formatively important. I suppose there is a good deal of self-indulgence in the exercise and possibly a sly wish to make my mark on the wall for posterity's dubious recognition. And certainly, one hopes that from this distant view some pattern might be discerned and that someone unknown to me, someone either in the failing light of middle age or in the dazzle of youth, facing his own problems in a different time and place, might find that pattern of relevance to his own condition.

THEN

In May 1945, I knew that my sister, Sylvia, who was five years younger than myself, had recently left her home in Aylesbury to live in Shepherd's Bush and at that time I knew no one else in London. I found the place where she lived, a flat in a fairly large block at the Holland Park end of the Green. When I rang the door bell a stranger answered, a short, compactly built young man with rather pale eyes which looked wary and unwelcoming. He wore a plaid shirt and old corduroy trousers. I asked him if my sister lived there. He was taking his time about answering when I heard her voice: 'Who's that, Cliff?' Then she appeared at his shoulder.

'Vernon! What are you doing here?' She turned to the young man. 'Cliff, this is my brother Vernon. You've heard me talk about him. This is Cliff. He's a painter.'

The caution disappeared from Cliff's eyes and he beamed. 'Glad to see you. Sylvia's told me a lot about you.'

I went into the flat which was impressively large, though I was soon to discover it was scarcely furnished at all. I was taken into the kitchen where a young man with a beard and a small dark girl were sitting at a table eating macaroni cheese. The girl was called Yvonne and she was an artist's model who had escaped from France at the beginning of the war and she had met Peter, the bearded fellow, at a concert a few months earlier—since when they had been living together in the flat. I saw that I had interrupted a meal and I apologized but Cliff assured me that there was plenty of food and invited me to join them. I sat down at the table and ate a plate of faintly cheese-flavoured macaroni and drank a cup of coffee. After the meal Peter and Yvonne left to go to a lecture and presently I got the chance to talk to Sylvia alone. I told her that I had deserted and would like to stay with her for a few days until I could get civilian clothes and find some way of earning a living. I hoped that Cliff would not be worried.

Sylvia laughed. 'Oh, Cliff won't mind. He'll be glad to help. He's on the run himself. So is Peter.'

The two young men were not on the run in quite the same way as I was. They were both registered as conscientious objectors and had been directed into work that was considered to be of national importance—Peter to a hospital to work as a porter and Cliff on to the land as a farm-labourer—but neither had obeyed the direction and they made a precarious living doing various jobs of doubtful legality. They both occasionally modelled at art schools but at that time Cliff had full-time work in an illicit factory for the making of dolls' heads. They were both Anarchists; Cliff passionately convinced of the truth of his convictions would quote Bakunin, Kropotkin and Herbert Read while Peter smiled with a gentle scepticism, non-committal, amused by his friend's enthusiasm. Cliff was in his mid-twenties but Peter, incredibly, was only nineteen, incredibly because, with his heavy black beard, he looked so much older and because in his short life he had acquired so much erudition and so many accomplishments.

He was almost entirely self-taught and he had learnt Latin with amazing ease and rapidity because he wanted to read Martial and distrusted translations. He could converse with Yvonne in her native tongue with complete fluency and he had read widely in English History and Literature. He had taught himself to play the piano and was a better than average performer. Sylvia told me that Cliff had one day returned to the flat from work and gone into the room that he used as a studio to find a freshly painted portrait of Peter on his easel. Cliff was annoyed that someone had used his paints and canvas but he was also intrigued, and even a little envious, for he admitted that the picture, while painted in a totally different idiom from the one he was trying to master, had been executed with a skill and assurance that was probably beyond his reach at that time. So, rather huffily, he asked Peter if he knew who had been painting in his studio.

'Oh, that,' said Peter. 'Hope you don't mind. I suddenly got the urge to try my hand at painting.'

Cliff could not at first believe it: Peter, who had never before touched a brush, had painted a more than respectable self-portrait at his first and, as far as I know, his only attempt.

If intelligence, taste, imagination and what seemed an effortless facility for mastering both creative and interpretative skills were sufficient to guarantee artistic achievement Peter would have become successful in one art or another, but there was a flaw in his temperament that made serious work impossible, a flaw that was perhaps an inevitable concomitant of the facility that seemed to me at that time so enviable: there was in him a fatal lack of seriousness. I do not mean, of course, that earnestness or solemnity is a necessary attribute of the artist; on the contrary, I doubt if a man who lacked wit and a sense of the comic could become an artist of real stature. But Peter's lack of seriousness was pervasive and finally emasculating. Although he read great literature and listened to great music— indeed, his taste would not accept anything inferior—his response to these experiences seemed inadequate. It was not simply a matter of reticence, of his not wishing to betray by outward signs the depth of his involvement; he was, in fact, uninvolved. He could attend a play or concert, read a poem or novel, taking pleasure in the artist's mastery of his medium, observing and approving it, yet never being transported, never being drawn into the heart of the work. His facial expression was always the same: ironic, smiling, sceptical, amused by the whole human comedy, amused, too, by the most transcendental achievements of the shaping imagination.

It would be easy to dismiss his uninvolvement as an act, a pretence of the cynicism—that world-weary shrugging off of life's variety— that is often affected by clever young people of undergraduate age; but with Peter it was not an affectation. He had been brought up in a lower middle-class environment. His widowed mother, whom he occasionally visited to cadge a small hand-out, ran a little café somewhere in the suburbs. His father, who had suffered from chronic mental illness, committed suicide and Peter had been removed from his grammar school at the age of fifteen in the unfulfilled expectation that he would help to support his mother. Almost immediately he left home and led a bum's existence, doing odd jobs when there was no other way of obtaining food and shelter. For a time he lived in somebody's tool-shed and each morning he would go to Covent Garden and buy or steal a few flowers which he would sell at the doors of housewives. His needs were simple enough. He dressed like a tramp, would eat anything that the human digestion could take, and seemed impervious to cold and physical discomfort.

Cliff was entirely different: he was not only an enthusiast but was, in his unmaterialistic way, very ambitious. He is now living, quite prosperously, in Sweden; he is still painting and still an enthusiast. I have not seen Peter since 1954 when I met him by chance in Notting Hill Gate after not having seen him for eight years or so. Physically he had not changed much though he had developed a disconcerting facial tic. He told me that he wandered about for a couple of years in France, Spain and Italy, had returned to England and somehow been awarded a scholarship to Oxford where he had taken a degree, taught for a couple of terms in a prep school, but was now unemployed again. I suggested that we should go for a drink but he refused. His smile was the same, gently derisive, but the tic, the sudden twitch of eyelid and facial muscle, was disturbing. When I asked him what had happened to Yvonne he was so vague that I wondered if he knew who I was talking about. There was always something very sad about Peter.

*

I was fitted out with civilian clothing of a kind. I was a lot bigger than either Cliff or Peter so there was nothing for it but to buy trousers. Sylvia supplied the necessary clothing coupons and I had enough cash to buy a pair of heavy workman's corduroys which Sylvia chose since I could not go into a civilian clothes shop dressed in uniform. Cliff parted with an old navy blue shirt, a useful colour since it would not show the dirt, and Peter dug out a discarded pair of sandals. The weather was fine and the whole of summer lay ahead. I would worry about getting a jacket later on.

And so began the first summer of my desertion, a time of excitement, anxiety and tentative growth. Everyone who has come from some other place to live in London, at whatever time, will preserve in memory those first impressions of his own personal city. My London of 1945 was fragmented: I became familiar with Shepherd's

Bush and Notting Hill Gate, Kensington Park Gardens and Speakers' Corner which I visited almost every Sunday afternoon. I got to know the literary and artistic 'Soho' of that time which in fact was not geographically in Soho at all but on the other side of Oxford Street, along Rathbone Place and into Charlotte Street where poets and painters drank in The Black Horse, The Wheatsheaf and The Fitzroy. Later I came to know Hampstead, Chalk Farm and Camden Town; and, later still, Bill Klein's gym in Fitzroy Square where, on autumn evenings, I would do a night's training and walk back through the misty, pungent thoroughfares to Monmouth Street where briefly I shared a room with a girl called Jackie.

Those earlier weeks are still bright in the memory with unfailing sunlight, the sense of liberation that was spiced by danger, the comfort of companionships that were not imposed by necessity, the enjoyment of listening to the talk of people whose thoughts dwelt on other things than booze and crumpet and how to work your ticket. I listened to music and nosed among the books that were scattered round the Shepherd's Bush flat. My reading was desultory but luxurious: a sip of Rilke, a large bite of Kafka, a bender on Baudelaire, a jig with MacNeice and banquets with Yeats and Auden. I was not getting down to the systematic reading I knew I needed but I was, as it were, limbering up and getting a lot of pleasure from it. They were good days, or so they seem to have been. Yet there were darker moments, too.

Cliff got me a job at the dolls' heads factory—though 'factory' is too imposing a name for that shed in a warehouse yard off the Euston Road where we worked for half-a-crown an hour boiling up the reeking mixture, whose ingredients I forget, if I ever knew them, and pouring it into moulds which were packed in tubs of ice until the heads had set to the consistency of soft damp rubber. The moulds, which were in two sections, were then split and the dolls' heads were placed on shelves in a strong current of air from an electric fan until they had dried and completely solidified. We then dusted them and filled in the pock-marks inflicted by the rough surfaces of the inside of the moulds, after which they were sprayed with paint and the eyes were painted in by Pat, the owner of the enterprise. It was not stimulating work but, without identity and unemployment cards, I was lucky to find any kind of job.

Pat was an ex-merchant seaman and he had no Board of Trade licence, or whatever authorization he was supposed to have for the manufacture of toys, and he paid us in cash without any deductions for income tax or unemployment stamps. At least he paid us in cash until he ran into difficulties when two of the firms he was supplying with heads failed to pay for consignments which had been delivered to them and he was forced to shut up shop. He owed us a fortnight's wages. He said he was very sorry but he could not give us what he did not possess—money—but what he did possess by the hundred was dolls' heads so we were paid off with two hundred of these each.

As soon as I started earning I left the flat in Shepherd's Bush and took a room for thirty shillings a week in Chalk Farm, but when my wages stopped and my landlady began to get restive I had to do a moonlight flit. Pat offered to put me up at his home in Hampstead until I found another job and he suggested that I might help his wife with her chores instead of paying rent. I was not much good at housework but I was useful in taking Pat's two children off his wife's hands for long periods. It was high summer and I would take the children—Kit, aged three, and Frankie aged five—on to the Heath for picnics, and in the evenings, after they were in bed, I would go for long solitary walks and feel a half painful, half luxurious loneliness when I saw young men out with their girls, carefree and respectable, or older married couples out for a stroll before returning to the substantial comforts of an established home. I no longer felt the reflex stab of apprehension at the sight of a policeman's uniform, which had troubled me in the first few weeks of my desertion, yet I was never entirely unaware of the precariousness of my freedom and I knew that I had only to be asked for my identity card and I would almost certainly be arrested and taken back to the Gordons' Depot for court martial and probably a long spell in the Glasshouse.

It was foolish of me to haunt the cafés and pubs of the raffish Charlotte Street area, but on the few occasions when I had enough cash for a beer I would make my way there and visit The Wheatsheaf or The Fitzroy and stand around, my loneliness intensified by the conviviality of the other drinkers, all of whom seemed to know each other well; yet this loneliness was not the unrelieved misery of the chronically and irredeemably solitary, the melancholy you so often see written on the faces of sad middle-aged drinkers in urban pubs: mine was a young man's loneliness, expectant, temporary, holding within it a vague promise of dissipation, of a marvellous encounter which would open the way into new and exciting territories. And encounters did occur, though they were never quite what the romantic imagination had, in its unfocused way, hoped for. The people I got into conversation with were not the luminaries who frequented those pubs, not the more or less well-known poets and painters, or the rich and mysterious beauties of a young man's fantasies, but displaced persons like myself, the young or not so young bums who today, I suppose, would be hippies. One of these was a young man who cherished an unlikely ambition to be a composer, unlikely because he seemed to have no practical knowledge of music and could neither, I suspected, play any instrument nor read a score. He worked back-stage in one of the West End theatres as a scene-shifter and he told me that I ought to be able to get similar work: I could dodge the problem of having no unemployment card by saying that I had another job and wanted part-time work in the evenings and I would be quite safe in claiming previous experience since the work was so simple.

One evening I met this acquaintance in Charlotte Street and he told me that he had heard that some one was wanted back-stage at the London Coliseum where a new show was about to open. The next morning I went round to the stage door and managed to get an interview with the man in charge of props.

'It's an electrician we want,' he said. 'You any good at electrics?'

I must have blenched because he said, 'Nothing to it really. It's Assistant Electrician. Sounds big stuff but you don't have to know nothing. Just work the spots and fix some fuses for the "Fire of Rome" scene. A baby could do it.'

I felt far from confident but I badly wanted to start earning again so I said I would like to have a shot and he told me to hang around and somebody would show me what the job was all about. Back-stage there was plenty of activity going on, great chunks of scenery being moved about and a lot of shouting and rancourless swearing. Presently a middle-aged little man wearing steel-rimmed glasses and a large cap came up to me and said, 'You're the young feller wanting the job, aren't you? Come along. I'll show you what you have to do.'

My duties seemed simple enough. The show was a fairly typical example of the kind of revue that was popular in the Forties, a mish-mash of unrelated sketches, solo-turns which were comic or senti-mental, all revolving round a 'star', in this case the comedian, Vic Oliver. In the opening number the chorus-boys had to go dancing on stage bearing different coloured lanterns on poles. I think they were supposed to be gondoliers but I am not certain. My job was to make sure that the bulbs inside the lanterns were all working and stand in the wings and hand a lantern to each of the chorus-boys as they passed. In the 'Fire of Rome' scene, in which Vic Oliver played a comic Nero, all I had to do was press a switch at the right moment which caused a short and in some way sent up clouds of harmless smoke which were played on by revolving red lights. There was a solo ballerina who had to be spotlighted and one or two other jobs, all perfectly simple and none of which required any electrical know-ledge at all, which was just as well since I possessed none. It was arranged that I would start the following Monday when the show opened.

My short life in show business was quite interesting at first but soon became very boring. The chorus girls would come dancing off stage into the wings, their huge smiles still fixed; then they would rush off to change from one flimsy costume to another and often one would rush up, smelling strongly of sweat and scent, and say, 'Fasten me up, dear, will you?' You would fumble at a hook or button and the girl would say 'ta' without looking at you, adjust her terrible smile and join the troupe to go, high-kicking, into the lights and applause. To them we, the stage-hands, were no more human than the props and equipment that we used.

My career in showbiz came to an end when I became over-confident in my ability to carry out my simple duties and I took to reading a book between the moments when I had a job to do. Vic Oliver had, I believe, trained as a musician before becoming a comedian and, for the finale, he abandoned the role of clown for that of maestro. Wearing tails, he would mount a specially high rostrum and conduct the orchestra as they pumped out some treacly Palm Court schmaltz. It was meant to be very serious and a brilliant white spotlight was focused on Oliver as the other lights were gradually dimmed. In the previous act I had used a crimson screen on my spotlight and, in my hurry to get back to my novel, I had forgotten to remove it. So when the great moment came, the conductor was not picked out by a shaft of white radiance but instead bathed in dramatic crimson which gave him a distinctly diabolical appearance. When I realized my mistake I snatched at the crimson screen but for some reason it stuck and, in my efforts to remove it, I tipped up the lamp; so that when at last a livid shaft of light was jetted into the darkness it missed Oliver, leaving him drowning in darkness, and hosed first on the chandeliers high above the audience and then straight into the dazzled stalls before I got it on target.

'Christ help you when he comes off, mate,' said one of my colleagues dispassionately.

I did not trust to divine help but turned and fled, never to return to that theatre or, in a professional capacity, to any other.

I had earned just over four pounds a week at the theatre, but I had built up debts which had to be paid off before I could think of renting another room so I was still living with Pat as a kind of not very helpful general help and I was feeling more and more conscious of being a parasite. Then I met Jackie.

I was walking along Oxford Street, feeling hungry and longing for a smoke, but I had no money for either food or tobacco. The late summer mellowness and the sexy gaiety of the girls in their light dresses, the wink and nod of brown flesh, the sense of purpose that motored the human and mechanical traffic, all mocked my own dejection and purposelessness. I knew that I ought to be searching the advertisement columns of the newspapers and the display cases of the newsagents for offers of some kind of work, but heat, hunger and fatigue had induced an inertia, a paralysis of the will to action. I was drifting. And then I bumped into someone, a girl. I mean I literally bumped into her. Perhaps the sun was in my eyes or her eyes; perhaps I was daydreaming; for whatever reason I collided with the girl who was walking quickly towards me and the bag of oranges she was carrying fell to the pavement and the fruit rolled into the gutter.

I apologized and scrambled to retrieve the oranges. When I straightened up and handed back her fruit, still apologizing, her expression of long-suffering patience suddenly disappeared and she looked quite friendly.

She said, 'I've seen you before, haven't I? Don't you go to The Wheatsheaf?'

I said that I did occasionally but I hadn't been there recently.

'Yes, I've noticed you. Usually on your own. Looking lost.'

'That sounds like me,' I said.

'What do you do?'

'Nothing at the moment, worse luck.'

'I mean do you write or paint or what?'

I told her I did none of these things, that I was just a man looking for a job.

She grinned. 'That makes a change, anyway. I thought all that lot were geniuses—poets, painters, novelists—that's what they'd like you to think.'

We were gradually being forced off the pavement by the main currents of movement.

She said, 'We can't talk here. Come and have a cup of tea.'

I felt embarrassed. 'I'm broke.'

She said, 'That doesn't matter. I meant let's go to my place. I can make a nice big pot there. I've got plenty of tea. Two chaps give me their ration.'

So I went to Jackie's place.

NOW

I DO not know whether it is possible to measure with any accuracy the quality of feelings that were experienced so long ago. Ensuing events impede the backward view. What, to an observer at the time, would seem the merest trivia of existence can later assume a magnitude, a poignancy, just as the seemingly mammoth experiences can erode in the countless rainfalls of the years. There are strange, involuntary infidelities of the heart and mind, particularly in erotic relationships. Past love-affairs change their colour, texture and fragrance, they are modified in the altering climate of subsequent encounters, and when, as I have now, it seems, settled for the exclusive local skirmishes, armistices and celebrations of marriage, it is more difficult than ever to recapture the flavour of those so distant affairs. Yet some objects of past love seem fixed and unchangeable, beyond the reach of corrosion, irreducible and still fresh, and I suspect that everyone possesses and treasures memories of these.

When people speak of 'first love' they usually mean the first conscious sexual experience, not necessarily fulfilled but recognized at the time as being related to certain positive biological urges; but one's first taste of the bitter-sweet fruit surely comes earlier and, while one is sharply aware of the turbulence, the joy and possible misery, one has no inkling of its real source and direction. I am not thinking in Freudian terms of infant sexuality but of that first mysterious and beautiful confrontation with someone who will continue to haunt the imagination for ever.

Of all the women I have known there are many, I am sure, who have been banished to the darkness of oblivion and there are others who must be dredged from the depths by deliberate or fortuitous associations or incantations. But there is that small company which is part of what I am myself, those women who are never totally absent from the consciousness. First, there is Sister Martin, whom I loved when I was four years old and living in Ballaghaderreen in Ireland where I attended the infants' school at the Convent, being too young to go to the Christian Brothers. Sister Martin was one of my teachers. She was gentle and she spoke and moved softly and her smile was immortal. My favourite game at home was playing at being Sister Martin. My father was a photographer and I would get hold of the black cloth that he put over his head when focusing his ancient studio camera and I would wear it as my coif, and my game was simply being Sister Martin. My love for her was pure: I did not wish to possess her. I wanted to be her.

There followed other loves as the libido was directed towards overt sexuality, the desire for fulfilment. There was Miss Steeples, my schoolteacher in Beeston, Nottinghamshire, when I was eight years old. She had beautiful finger-nails and smelled like Boots Cash Chemists. I would haunt the environs of the tennis club where she sometimes played on summer evenings and on treasured occasions I would see her, coming or going, golden in the sunlight, negligently swinging a netted catch of tennis balls. Whatever conquests Miss Steeples might have made, none was more complete than her domination of my small heart.

Later, when I was fourteen, came Doris who was a year older than myself. I saved my pocket-money for weeks to buy her a pendant which looked like a sucked pear-drop attached to a frail chain. After we had been for many walks along the canal tow-path, held hands and practised kissing, she at last let me play with her naked and—unless memory deceives—remarkably well-developed breasts. I suffered refinements of pleasure and torment over her and when she abandoned me for a bank clerk with a Morris Cowley I spent weeks in a state of misery and despair that even now, however faintly, reverberates down the years. She was plump and effervescent and generous and I am sure I must have bored her with my priggishness and clumsiness.

I must have bored Angela, too, who at twenty-six and eight years older than me, had the very doubtful pleasure of taking my reluctantly preserved virginity. She was small, nubile and promiscuously passionate. I had not the sense to value what she generously offered but needs must change her to some sentimental ideal of a woman: I tried to get her to read poetry and the D. H. Lawrence novels and stories that I was then devouring. I preached her addle-pated sermons on poetry and revolution. It is amazing that she put up with my nonsense for as long as she did.

But I must stop this maundering. I must get back to Jackie who was very good to me; yet I do not remember her vividly as I do the women I have been thinking about. Perhaps this is because she did not cause me any pain. I remember her straight fair hair and her blue eyes which showed a curious mixture of candour and deceit. I wish I could tell her that I liked her very much and admired her courage and recklessness, but she is dead now. She died a few years ago and I did not learn of her death until some time afterwards when a man, who also lived with her for a time, casually mentioned it as we were having a drink in a Soho pub and talking about old times.

THEN

I MOVED in with Jackie. Her flat was in Monmouth Street and she shared it with two men, each of whom had his room, and all three shared the kitchen. There was no bathroom but the Holborn Public Baths were close-by. One of the men who shared the flat was a Ceylonese writer of very short short stories; he was gentle and charming and unsuccessful. The other was a witty and intelligent Welshman with a crippling stammer which prevented him from finding the academic job that his qualifications and temperament fitted him for.

Jackie had the largest room and it was quite well furnished. There were plenty of books about and she had a record-player and a wildly mixed selection of records: lots of Sinatra, some traditional jazz and a few of the more popular 'classics', some Mozart, the Beethoven Fifth and Seventh Symphonies and the Fourth and Fifth Piano Concertos, some Ravel and the César Franck Violin Sonata. Things were looking up.

I told her about the two hundred dolls' heads which were stored in Pat's garden shed in Hampstead.

'We'll get them,' she said. 'I'll make bodies and dresses for them. I can borrow a sewing-machine.'

When I went to Pat's to collect my few belongings and to tell him I was leaving, Jackie came with me. We hired a taxi to carry the large case of dolls' heads and as soon as we got back to the flat she started to design bodies and dresses for the finished dolls she was determined to make. She worked very hard for four days and completed a couple of dozen dolls; then her enthusiasm was extinguished, abruptly and totally.

'I'm fed up,' she said. 'How do we get rid of them?'

I said that Christmas was not so very far away and, though the

Japanese had by now been defeated, neither they nor the Germans would be exporting toys for a long time to come. Any toyshop would snap up our dolls.

'Okay,' Jackie said. 'I've done the work. You go and flog the things. You're the firm's sales force.'

That did not appeal to me at all. I had told Jackie on our first meeting that I was on the run from the Army, information that did not in the least distress her or even seem of much interest.

I said, 'I can't possibly go into toyshops with a few home-made dolls. They'd think I'd pinched them. Somebody would be sure to put the cops on to me.'

'Okay,' she said cheerfully. 'Let's take a few round the pubs tonight. See if we can get rid of them that way.'

And that is what we did. In the evening we put half a dozen dolls into a carrier bag and went out early to catch the businessmen who dropped into the pub for a quick one on the way home. We found that we could sell them without trying. The heads, staring with their stunned blue eyes over the lip of the bag, immediately attracted attention and we soon got rid of the batch at twelve shillings and sixpence each. We enjoyed a week or so of affluence, eating and drinking well, and then we were again without money, with a month's rent due to be paid. I felt guilty at not being able to earn anything and while Jackie, who was used to supporting parasitical men, did not criticize, the feeling of humiliation grew stronger as days went by. So I went to Shepherd's Bush to see if Cliff had any suggestions to make.

He said I had arrived at the right time. He was about to start a new enterprise which would operate on Saturdays only. He had bought very cheaply a couple of gallons of perfume from an Indian acquaintance who had also supplied him with a quantity of little scent bottles. I was to help him to fill the bottles and accompany him early on Saturday morning to Walthamstow Market where he had rented a stall. At three-and-six a bottle the stuff should sell to the ladies of Walthamstow like iced lager in hell. We would work on the stall together in the morning but in the afternoon I would be left in sole charge because Cliff had an appointment. He would pay me twenty per cent of the day's takings.

The following Saturday was fine and sunny, the last really warm day of an Indian summer, and we had fixed up our stall and set out our display of bottles of scent by ten in the morning. Out of sight we had a carton full of empty bottles and a jar of perfume to fill them from when we ran out of stock. But trade was slow in starting and by mid-morning we had sold only three bottles. Cliff was less inhibited than I. He would imitate the other vociferous stall-holders and bawl out, 'Exotic perfumes from the East! Lovely perfume, only three-and-six a bottle! Costs you thirty shillings in the shops! Lovely perfume!'

When a policeman walked past I moved away from the stall and tried to look as if I had no connection with it or with Cliff who carried on shouting his wares with obstinate enthusiasm. By lunch time we had sold another five bottles and the sun was throbbing steadily in a clear sky and the heat was making the sickly fumes of our merchandise almost unbearably strong. Cliff said he would see me back at the flat at Shepherd's Bush and off he went to keep his appointment. Shortly afterwards, a group of factory girls, just released for the weekend, approached the stall and I looked at them with hopeful invitation as one of them paused and stared back at me. Then she said, almost with awe, 'My Gawd, what a stink!' She hurried on to catch up with her friends and I saw them look back at my stall and then I heard shrill laughter.

I was ready to pack up and go except that I would have been ashamed to face Cliff without having made any more sales. Then a girl of about fifteen bought a bottle and I ate the meat pie I had brought with me for my lunch and drank thirstily from the bottle of beer that Cliff had provided. After I had eaten, business did begin to improve and a surprising number of girls and women invested in the terrible stuff I was dispensing. The reek of the scent gradually seemed to permeate every pore of my body and even find its way down my throat and into the stomach. I thought I would never be free of the taste of it.

By five o'clock I had had enough and I packed up what was left of my goods into the old cardboard suitcase Cliff had used that morning and I set off back to Shepherd's Bush. I received some astonished and hostile stares in the underground train but I was too sick and tired to care. The day's work earned me thirty-four shillings, less fares, and I did not work as a perfume vendor again.

*

Somehow Jackie and I managed to pay the rent and eat fairly regularly. She was adept at finding new sources of loans and she was pretty unscrupulous at exploiting them. She often called on an elderly aunt in St. John's Wood and she never came back from these visits without a pound or two. I began by thinking that the old lady gave her little presents of money but, when I commented on the aunt's generosity, Jackie laughed and shamelessly admitted that she filched the money either from the old girl's purse or from a silver teapot which was used as a home savings bank.

Then suddenly the summer was over. I had no memory of its softening into autumn, though I suppose it must have done. After grey and windy days the nights were sharp with rumours of winter and expensively spiced with the smoke of cigars. The shop windows slopped yellow light on to the pavements and the air tingled with cold. In Charlotte Street the taxis eased to the kerb outside the more elegant restaurants and you would hear the careless voices, the enviable laughter of privilege, rank and security on the night air, flavouring it like the aroma of rich food. In The Fitzroy Tavern the piano would pound away at tunes which had no power to move me then but can now touch places in the heart that would not be accessible to much nobler music, and in the street outside The Wheatsheaf a piano-accordion squeezed out its vulgar and seductive lamentations. Luckily Pat had given me an old tweed jacket and a woollen sweater from his seaman's days or I would have perished.

It was in November that I thought of a possible way of making some money. Jackie and I were in a pub in Covent Garden sitting gloomily over two half pints of bitter, which was all we could afford, when I noticed a copy of the weekly paper, *Boxing News*, lying on the bar. I asked the barman if I could have a look at it and when I turned to the back pages I saw an advertisement placed there by someone called Wally Dakin: it said that he was willing to manage

27

any young amateur boxer of proven ability who wished to turn professional and that he could be contacted at Bill Klein's gymnasium at an address in Fitzroy Square.

I said, 'That's it, Jackie! I can make a few quid there.'

She looked startled. 'Boxing! What do you know about boxing?'

'Enough. I'll go and see Wally Dakin tomorrow.'

She needed some convincing that I was serious and, after I had assured her that I had boxed a good deal and knew something about the game, she objected: 'But even if they let you do it, it would be crazy. You'd be in the public eye, wouldn't you? Somebody would recognize you and that would be that.'

I told her I did not think so. I would use a phoney name and, since I did not expect to be involved in anything more ambitious than a preliminary six-rounder in one of the small halls, I would be unlikely to attract much attention.

'It's one of the few things I do quite well,' I said. 'And you don't need cards for this job. It's made for me. I even like it.'

So the next morning I walked to Fitzroy Square and found Bill Klein's gymnasium. You went down some stone steps into a basement area and the gym was a single large room with a ground level ring, a couple of heavy punch-bags and a speed ball. Changing accommodation and a single shower were partitioned off from the main room. At the end farthest from the entrance was a counter at which you could buy a cup of tea. There were posters on the walls advertizing fights that were shortly to take place and I could smell the familiar and exciting pungency of massage oils. Two lightweights were sparring in the ring wearing headguards and big training gloves, a heavier man was thumping on one of the bags and a coloured fighter, heavily sweatered, was skipping expertly.

Bill Klein was behind the counter, a small monosyllabic man in late middle age wearing a dirty white sweater and an unfriendly expression.

I asked for Wally Dakin.

'Not been in.'

'Do you know where I'd be likely to find him?'

'You a fighter?' He looked sceptical.

I said, 'Amateur, want to turn pro.'

He looked even more sceptical. Then he said grudgingly, 'He lives over the road,' and he gave me the number of the house.

I left the gym and crossed the road to the row of secretive tall houses opposite and rang the bell at the number I had been given. A few moments later the door opened and a tall dark-haired man with a thin moustache and asymmetrical features said, 'Yeah?'

I said I was looking for Wally Dakin.

'You've found him.'

'I saw your advertisement in *Boxing News*. I thought I'd like to turn pro.'

He looked a little less sceptical than Bill Klein, but not much. 'Oh.' He looked me up and down and then said without much enthusiasm, 'Okay, come on up.'

I went into the house and followed him up the stairs to a small, sparsely-furnished bedroom. He sat on the bed and waved towards the single straight-backed chair. 'Have a seat.'

He got out a tin of tobacco and rolled himself a cigarette. 'What do they call you?' he said.

I was ready for this. 'Bain,' I said. 'John Bain.'

'Johnny Bain . . . yeah, that sounds all right. You want to keep your name if you fight pro?'

'Yes, I think so.'

'You've boxed amateur, have you? What club?'

I told him the name of the club I had boxed for before the war and added that I had also boxed in the Army before I had been discharged.

'Won any titles?'

'Finalist in the British Schoolboys' Championships, North West Divisional Junior Champion. The war stopped me going in for the Senior A.B.A.s.'

'What's your weight?'

'About eleven-six, middle.'

He asked me many more questions: the names of men I had fought in the amateurs and in the Services, had I won many fights by a knock-out, had I been knocked out. As my answers showed at least some familiarity with the game he became much more friendly and began to talk about fighters he had managed in the past and of his ambition to find a really good one he could guide to the top.

'The best I had', he said, 'was Frank Hough. You remember Frank?'

I remembered Hough, a middleweight, an ex-regular Guardsman who had been a competent rather than inspiring professional.

'I thought I'd got a world-beater there, but he hadn't quite got it.'

Before we parted we arranged that I should meet him in the gym that evening and he would bring along someone for me to box a couple of rounds with. After that he would decide whether or not he would take me on as a professional fighter.

'I'll give it to you straight, Johnny,' he said. 'That's the best way for both of us. No use kidding around. If you've got what it takes, okay, I'll tell you so. If you haven't, the same thing goes. I'll tell you straight. Coupla rounds and I'll be able to tell. This Irish kid I'll put you in with, he's a useful trial horse. But that's all he's good for. If you can't handle him you'll never handle anybody. Okay?'

I said I would be there that evening at seven o'clock. Then I hurried back to Monmouth Street and told Jackie I had to have some kit for the evening. The Ceylonese writer had just been paid for a script he had done for the BBC Overseas Service so we were able to borrow a couple of pounds and go to Gamage's Sports Department where I bought the cheapest pair of boxing-boots they had and a pair of trunks. Next, I bought some gutta-percha from a chemist so that I could make myself a gumshield, a fairly crude one, it is true, but much better than none at all.

I was nervous on my way to the gym. I had not boxed for over a year and I knew that my timing would be poor, but this concerned me less than my physical condition. For the past six months my meals had been irregular and often scanty. I had taken no exercise more strenuous than walking and I doubted whether I would be able to last more than a round or two before my wind was spent and my arms and legs began to fill with lead. As I passed the pubs and cafés I began to wonder whether I had not been fooling myself about my ability to hold my own against a professional and I thought with envy of the people at the bars or tables carelessly eating and drinking without a thought for the consequences.

The gym was much busier than it had been in the morning. More than a dozen boxers were working outside the ring, bag-punching, shadow-boxing, skipping or doing abdominal exercises on the floor. Wally Dakin was standing at the counter talking to Bill Klein. I joined him and he said to Klein, 'This is the boy I was telling you about. Give him a card, Bill. I'll pay his sub.' He turned to me. 'Go and get stripped, son. If you've got any cash or a watch I'll look after it for you.'

I told myself that if I had any cash or a watch I would not be where I was and I went behind the partition to change into my embarrassingly new-looking gear. When I rejoined Dakin he looked at me with a dealer's judicial scrutiny and said, 'You don't look in bad shape. A bit of suet round the middle's got to come off.'

I said, 'I'll have to take it easy to start with. I'm right out of training.'

'We'll soon fix that. Start you nice and easy. A couple of rounds sparring, a couple on the bag and a couple with the rope. A bit of groundwork and that'll do you for tonight.'

I thought it would probably kill me, but I did not say so.

He said, nodding towards the ring, 'You know those two?'

I looked at the two boxers who were sparring. One of them looked familiar. 'Isn't that . . .'

'Danahar and Odwell. You watch Arthur. Lovely moves. Watch 'em both. Teach you a lot.'

I remembered Arthur Danahar of Bethnal Green. We had boxed on the same bill before the war when he was an amateur and one of the finest lightweights to win an A.B.A. title. Then he had been a slim pale boy in his teens but now he had filled out into a chunky muscular welterweight and his style had changed from a loose, more open stance to a compact, completely functional style, both gloves held high, elbows close in to protect the body. He seemed to move without effort, slipping left leads with an almost casual flick to one side of the head and countering with fast, piston-like shots to the body and head. When the man who was keeping time called out to end the round, Danahar did not appear even to be breathing heavily.

The two boxers left the ring and Dakin said, 'Let's have a set of gloves, Bill. See what this boy can do.' He called to a red-haired boxer who was exercising on the floor, 'Come on Paddy, get the gloves on!'

Paddy was lean and bony; he had the kind of physique that is more serviceable than beautiful, hard, angular and durable. Dakin laced on our gloves and we got into the ring. My mouth was dry and currents of excitement and apprehension travelled over the nerves and moved queasily in the stomach. Dakin held a stop-watch in his hand.

He called, 'Okay. First round . . . time!'

As soon as I shaped up, the nervous tension disappeared. I tried a couple of left jabs and a hook to the body that connected with one of Paddy's bony elbows. Paddy retaliated, swinging wildly with both hands. I knew straight away that he was the worst kind of fighter to spar with. He was crude, clumsy and unorthodox, and he did not react to feints or shifts in any predictable way. It was not that he was undeceived but he was entirely unaware of his opponent's strategy. Whatever tactics you adopted he simply charged forward with great lunges and swings, happy enough to take half a dozen stiff punches if he could connect with one solid haymaker and get in close and bang away at your ribs.

The trouble with that kind of fighter is that he can make you look almost as bad as himself. An opponent in the ring is, in a way, rather like a dancing-partner. If he moves well, fluently and intelligently, your own performance is likely to match his. Sparring with Paddy was like dancing with a cart horse. I knew I was not looking impressive though I did catch Paddy with one solid right-cross that made his eyes roll upward as if he were invoking heavenly aid, but the only real benefit I gained from the two rounds was the knowledge that I was not so badly out of condition as I had feared.

As Dakin was removing my gloves I said, 'I know I looked terrible. He's awkward. I couldn't get going.'

'You did all right. You've got a nice left jab and that was a good right hand you caught him with. Your timing wants sharpening up and you was out of distance with the left hook but we'll fix all that. Paddy's an awkward bugger, I know. Now get some mittens on and we'll have a go at the bag.'

The next evening I sparred three rounds with Paddy and did more skipping, groundwork and bag-punching. My timing was better and I found I could catch Paddy with the right-cross almost at will. Dakin was pleased with the way I was shaping and he told me that a friend of his was putting on a show at Ipswich and he would find an opponent for me to make one of the six-round preliminary bouts.

I won my first professional fight quite easily though I was given a shock in the first round when I walked into a right hand from my opponent, a roughish but not very skilled boxer from Romford, and found myself on the canvas. I took a count of eight, by which time my mind was quite clear again. I made sure that there was no repetition of the knock-down by keeping my man at a distance with a long left jab and making a lot of use of the ring. In the second round I kept the left jab going but followed up with an occasional short right to the chin and a left hook to the body and it was this combination of punches that put the Romford boy down in the fourth round. He got up at the count of seven but he was still shaken so I sent him back to the canvas with a left hook to the head. He was struggling to get up when the referee stopped the fight.

I was paid five pounds and my travelling expenses and ten shillings of this was deducted by an official from the Boxing Board of Control to pay for the licence that every professional boxer must possess, but Dakin did not ask for his manager's cut which I thought was nice of him since he could not have been very well off.

I had two more six-rounders during the next few weeks, one at the Lime Grove Baths and one at Watford Town Hall and I won them both on points against pretty poor opposition. Another promotion was being arranged at Ipswich and Dakin said that he would fix me up with my first eight-rounder, but this contest never took place, for something happened that was to change the entire course of my life. In The Fitzroy Tavern one Saturday evening I met a medical student from Leeds who was in London for a few days to take an examination.

Details of the meeting have faded but I must have drunk a good deal for I was indiscreet enough to tell him—probably boastfully—that I was on the run from the Army. He said that I was crazy to stay in London where the police were always on the look-out for deserters. Only the other night he had seen a Black Maria pull up outside a Soho café and cart off most of the patrons. Sooner or later I was sure to be asked for my identity-card. Why not go north, to Leeds? I would find the cost of living cheaper and he was sure I would be able to get work of some kind. Perhaps I had a misguided notion of what Leeds was like. People from down south seemed to think it was nothing but factories, fish-and-chip shops and Rugby League football. Not at all. It was culturally stimulating. There was a university, regular symphony concerts at the Town Hall, lunch-time recitals at the museum, a repertory cinema and a theatre where first-class companies tried out first-class plays before the London run. There were plenty of civilized people. Away from the flashy distractions of the metropolis I would be able to concentrate on being a writer, if that—as I had told him—was what I wanted to be.

I said that he was right; I would go to Leeds. And the surprising thing is that the idea really took root and was not dismissed the next morning as a drunken fantasy. When I spoke to Jackie about going she agreed that I might be safer there but she herself could not imagine living anywhere but in London. I, on the other hand, had lived in Lancashire as a child and I had affectionate memories of the north. And I had a strong and only partly conscious reason for going away: I knew that I was living with Jackie under false pretences. I liked her well enough but I certainly did not love her, nor did I even find her physically attractive, so our relationship was a demoralizing one. She cried for a while when I said I was definitely going, but then she cheered up and said, 'You'll be back inside three weeks. But don't be surprised if I've got another boy-friend by then.'

*

I arrived in Leeds on a misty evening and the cold was damp and pervasive. I carried all my possessions in a carrier-bag and in my pocket I had three pounds and some small change. My medical student friend met me and we had a beer in a pub on Briggate and some fish and chips at a place near the medical school and then we went to his digs where I spent the night shivering on his floor under a thin blanket and a couple of coats. The next day he sent me to

Francis Street in the Chapeltown district where he had been told there was a cheap room to let. The address he gave me turned out to be the headquarters of the North Leeds Communist Party, a decaying three-storied building with an attic which was the advertised vacant room. The caretaker's wife showed me to the attic which was furnished with a camp bed, a table, two chairs and an oil stove.

She said, 'It's not up to much but it's only seven-and-six a week. You can get a few bits and pieces and make it more homely. No linen but there's three good blankets on the bed, clean too. You use the lav and wash-basin on the floor below.'

I said it would suit me fine and I paid her a week's rent and told her I would be moving in later in the day. She gave me a key to the front door and said she hoped I would be comfortable and I went back to the medical student's place, picked up my carrier bag, walked the couple of miles or so back to Francis Street and went up to the attic. It looked very bare but I was pleased with it. I thought it would be quite inviting once I had collected a few books and hung some bright reproductions on the walls.

The medical student, on his own ground and busy with his work and friends with their specialized interests, quickly lost interest in me and my circumstances. I suppose a situation that had seemed slightly bizarre and exciting in London simply lost its piquancy now that he was back in his own *milieu*. I did not blame him for his cooling off and I was determined not to make a nuisance of myself, so we did not see much of each other once I was established in Francis Street, though he did give me a useful present—a thick university scarf which, as he said, would lend me a kind of respectability and superficial identity as well as helping to keep the cold wind out.

My relationship with Leeds was like some love affairs: I began by finding the place ugly but fascinating, and gradually came to perceive, in that gaunt and variegated city, beauties that could not be rivalled by the cleaner features of places conventionally more handsome. But there were moments of estrangement when I felt the city to be indifferent, if not positively hostile; moments of nostalgic longing for the consolations of London.

At first I was very lonely. I would walk the streets and hear the voices about me, the vowels slapping out hard and flat, the un-accustomed rhythms and idioms, and I would feel excluded, alien. Christmas was close and the air tingled with festive anticipation that seemed maliciously to taunt me with my loneliness. The convivial noises from the bars I could not afford to enter, the laughter and the singing, the friendships and the kissing, all pro-vided food for my fattening self-pity, and there were times when I thought I could not stay in Leeds any longer, that I would hitch-hike south, returning to a London which at these moments seemed warm, welcoming and maternal. Yet something kept me there and when I had survived the intense loneliness of my frugal Christmas I began to search for work.

The medical student had suggested a possible way of making some money: there were lots of parents, he said, who were des-perately anxious that their children should not fail to win a place in the Grammar School or High School. These parents had not enough money to educate their children privately yet they could afford to pay a tutor to give personal tuition in the evenings or at weekends.

'You look in the *Evening Post*. You'll see plenty of people advertis-ing for a tutor.'

I told him that I had no qualifications, that I had not even been to a Grammar School myself, but he swept my objections aside.

'Don't be silly. Who's to know what qualifications you've got or haven't got. Tell 'em you've got a degree. You'd be safe enough if you said you'd got an English degree. Then all you've got to do is swot up a bit on what you're supposed to be teaching the kid. After all, the youngster wouldn't need coaching if he was bright, would he? All you've got to do is keep one jump ahead of a dull ten-year-old. That shouldn't be too difficult.'

At first I did not take the suggestion very seriously but when I found that my small supply of money had almost run out I recon-sidered the possibility of doing some private coaching. My hesitation was not the consequence of moral scruples but fear of being un-covered as an impostor and exposed to ridicule or worse. But the risk had to be taken since I could think of no other way of earning a living. I began to search the small advertisements of the *Yorkshire Evening Post* and on the third day of looking I found someone

36

asking for a teacher to give private lessons in English and arithmetic to a nine-year-old girl. I wrote at once to the box number and said that I was a graduate of London University who had taught for a couple of years but now wished to escape from the routine of a regular job in order to devote myself to writing. I could, however, spare a few hours each week for private coaching and I would gladly undertake the tuition of the little girl for a fee of ten shillings an hour.

I received a reply by return of post from a Mr James Andrews asking me to call at an address in a middle-class residential area on the outskirts of Leeds, and there I went, clad in my appalling best clothes, to be interviewed for the job. Mr Andrews was a Scotsman, a former ship's engineer who was now in charge of the plant at a large clothing manufacturers, and I found that he was even more nervous than I and, although he had that almost superstitious reverence for learning that is often found among the Scots, especially those who have not themselves enjoyed the best of educations, he knew even less about scholastic matters than I did. He was very shy, good-humoured and found it hard to talk about money but it was finally agreed that I should come twice a week in the evening and I would be paid ten shillings on each visit plus my bus fares. There was no mention of my being expected to supply references.

Anne, my pupil, was a pretty and intelligent little girl, mercifully weak enough at arithmetic for me to be able to appear proficient, fond of reading and responsive to suggestions for composition. I enjoyed the lessons and found to my surprise that I was quite a good teacher. I also discovered that a highly effective method of learning an unfamiliar subject is to teach it. For instance my knowledge of formal English grammar was nugatory before I was confronted with the task of teaching Anne how to parse and analyse sentences, but I rapidly acquired a thorough familiarity with the hitherto mysterious language of case, mood, voice and tense and could soon take to pieces the most elaborate sentence and describe with confidence the precise function and nature of each of its clauses. The value of such exercises is, I suppose, debatable, but Anne and I enjoyed doing them and at least she gained in confidence for she had never been able to understand these mysteries when they had been taught in class, and she had blamed her own stupidity.

37

After our first lesson I was invited to stay to supper; the invitation was repeated every time I visited and the meals became a very important addition to my fee. Mrs Andrews was a warm, gay little woman, a good and inventive cook whose meals were treats to look forward to. All food was rationed at that time, though for the wealthy there was plenty served in restaurants. On my income of one pound a week and with no ration-book things were difficult. The British Restaurant in the bowels of the Town Hall served substantial midday meals of toad-in-the-hole or shepherd's pie for about one-and-sixpence and there were plenty of fish-and-chip shops, but I could not patronize these very often with only twelve-and-six— once the rent had been paid—to satisfy all my needs for a week.

I kept my eye on the *Yorkshire Evening Post* advertisements and soon I found more work coaching the young, though nothing so pleasant as my job with Anne. I gave a lesson in English language and literature to a boy in Headingley at weekends and three evenings each week I coached a girl in Roundhay. This was a tricky one. The advertisement had said: *Tutor wanted for girl 11. General subjects.* When I went for the interview it was the mother I saw, a stout and flint-eyed lady who was clearly suspicious of my uncouth appearance which I had hoped might just pass as the careless, bohemian dress of the eccentric academic. Her daughter, Karen, who was a smaller and not much more attractive version of herself, had just moved from a state school to an independent fee-paying establishment in Harrogate where she was expected to grapple with French, Latin and algebra.

I said that I was an arts man and could not undertake to teach mathematics so I was hired to instruct Karen in French, Latin and English. I accepted the job, partly because I could not turn down thirty shillings a week and, just as important, because I could not, as a putative graduate of London University, confess that I did not know a word of either French or Latin. I arranged that our first lesson would be English and this gave me three days to learn enough French and Latin to begin teaching Karen. I prayed that the child was as stupid as she looked and, luckily for me, she was; so I was able to conceal my ignorance of the subjects I was supposed to have mastered and I actually succeeded in passing on to her my own exiguous but steadily increasing knowledge of them.

When I began my course of self-instruction with the help of school grammars and those seductive Teach Yourself books, borrowed and repeatedly renewed from the public library, I found that my five years of mental inactivity in the Army had not, as I had feared, robbed me of the power to learn; on the contrary they seemed to have generated a vast intellectual appetite, a hunger that increased as it was fed, and I was surprised by the ease with which I could memorize detail. I slogged really hard at my French and Latin and I also began to read more systematically in English; no longer did I go in for those promiscuous flirtations with books that I had pursued in London but I formed a deep and passionate devotion to them, and, although I was still wandering through the forests, plains and mountains of literature without guide, map or compass, I was beginning to have some vague idea of the way these territories might be charted.

I read criticism, fiction and poetry, perhaps more poetry than anything else. There are still books on my shelves that I acquired in Leeds: the Home University Library anthology of sixteenth- and seventeenth-century poetry in which I first enjoyed Henry King, Marvell, Herbert and Donne; a 1943 edition of Matthew Arnold's Poems of Wordsworth, picked up second-hand for two shillings; the Faber Selected Poems of Auden and the Collected Poems of Edward Thomas. And it was then, in early 1946, that I first read the novels of Dostoevsky, Hardy and Melville. Somehow I stumbled across Djuna Barnes's *Nightwood* and William Faulkner's *The Sound and the Fury*, heady stuff on an empty stomach. By the same blind luck I found in the public library I. A. Richards' *Principles of Literary Criticism* and was led on to Coleridge, Hopkins, Eliot and Yeats. Again by chance, I found Hart Crane's poems and was dazzled, bewildered and excited by them. I started to write poems of my own, and singularly bad they were, too, though mercifully I did not at the time realize how awful. Life was charged with wonder and danger and promise.

There were times when books no longer sufficed, when my loneliness craved for human company; in fact the intensity of pleasure that reading provided also generated a need to share that pleasure with another person, and soon I was lucky enough to find someone who was able, not only to share my excitement in literature, but to advise and to some extent to direct my reading and correct the more outrageous faults in my writing.

I was doing enough coaching to pay my rent, eat frugally and buy an ounce and a half of tobacco each week for rolling cigarettes and still have left over about ten shillings for books, clothes, shoe-repairs and so on. On the whole I was able to discipline myself quite firmly but every now and then I would rebel, dig into my small savings and go into the city centre on a pub crawl. One evening I was in a pub in an alley off Briggate which was used by a heterogeneous crowd of journalists, punters, con men, students and indefinables when a voice at my side said, 'Hullo, you're at the University, aren't you? I haven't seen you around the Union.'

A young man of about my own age was smiling in a friendly way. He had thick black hair, worn very long at a time and in a place where most men favoured short back and sides. His eyes and complexion were unusually dark, Spanish-looking, and he stooped a little, like a man of greater height. I avoided giving a direct answer about my being at the University by asking him what he was studying there. His name was Kenneth Severs and he was a post-graduate student working—or rather failing to work—on a PhD thesis on twentieth-century poetic drama. He also edited a little magazine called the *Northern Review* and he wrote poetry.

We were an oddly contrasting couple yet in many ways we complemented each other. Kenneth had suffered a serious spinal injury as a child and had not been fit to serve in the Armed Forces, but neither had he led a cloistered life for he had worked as a reporter on a northern daily before going up to the University to take a first in English. He was incomparably better read than I was and his tastes were more sophisticated. Through his example I learnt to cut out the more blatant romantic excesses in the stuff I was writing and it was he who introduced me to Bonamy Dobrée, who was then the Professor of English at Leeds, George Wilson Knight, who had just joined the staff, and some of the extra-mural literati among the Leeds bohemian fringe which included the poet and playwright, R. C. Scriven, and the painter, Jacob Kramer.

That winter was like a military campaign; mist and fog would blind the city in yellowish grey like poison gas; sleet and snow put down their barrage to the muffled echoes of bursting pipes; the roads and pavements were booby-trapped with ice, and north-easters waited at every street corner to bayonet you. At night the trams spat blue sparks overhead and you heard their metallic stomping as they moved off to the wastelands of Beeston or Belle Isle or to the pudding-fed respectability of Headingley and Roundhay. I shivered over my oil stove and piled on to my camp bed whatever coverings I could lay hands on. Then the winter was suddenly over and the city was beautiful with barrows of daffodils bright yellow against the black and grey stone of the streets and buildings and the girls in summer frocks, gay and gossamer as butterflies, floating down the Headrow towards the big shops. Boys in the parks or on waste ground played serious games of cricket, using their heaped jackets for wickets and, in the lucky gardens of the posh, laburnum melted and dripped.

I was still finding enough coaching to keep me alive and I was working at my poems and reading with undiminished appetite. I had begun to send my work out to the magazines but the poems always came back with printed rejection-slips until one morning the literary editor of *Tribune* accepted one. A few weeks later Middleton Murry, who at that time edited the *Adelphi*, took two poems and, better still, since the payment was generous, the Chicago journal, *Poetry*, decided to print a couple. I was delighted and believed, quite mistakenly, that this was the beginning of a successful literary career.

On Sundays I would often go to Roundhay Park and watch the visiting county cricket eleven playing a one-day match against a scratch team that often included great players of the past whose names I remembered from cigarette cards. In the evenings, if I stayed in my room, I would often be troubled by the old ache of loneliness and there were times when I longed to be free of the continuous, though usually mild, itch of anxiety about the illegality of my position. What worried me as much as the danger of being picked up was the constant need for vigilance and for dissimulation. I could not tell the truth about my predicament, partly because I knew it would be foolish to spread around the information that I was a deserter but also because it would be unfair to burden others with anxiety or force upon them a crisis of conscience. I did not tell Kenneth that I was on the run but at times I hinted at it and I believe he guessed something very close to the truth.

Before the next academic year began I asked Bonamy Dobrée if it would be possible for me to attend some of his lectures and he generously arranged that I should go to any lecture I wished and also that I could join one of Wilson Knight's tutorial groups. I had to pay a quite modest fee which included the Union subscription so I was able to make use of the Union cafeteria, the baths, reading-room and other facilities. I also joined the University Boxing Club.

Strictly speaking, since I had boxed professionally, even for so brief a period, I could not claim amateur status without a full enquiry by the A.B.A., and official reinstatement, but it seemed unlikely that my defection would be discovered. So one autumn night I went round to the University gym and watched the boxing team training for a forthcoming match with Cambridge. The standard of university boxing is very low. Like the public schools the universities tend to produce a type of clumsy slogger who seems to take a pride in looking more like a rugger player than a boxer. Boxing, like soccer, is a proletarian game, a sport that is more theatrical than most and which requires of the accomplished per-former that he should not only be skilful, resourceful and dangerous, but that he should look these things, too. It is not that the first-class boxer must have histrionic ability or exhibitionist tendencies—though he sometimes has—but that it is virtually impossible to execute really effective moves without looking like a mixture of expert swordsman and dancer. Reticence and good form have no place in the ring. Boxing is not an occupation for gentlemen.

The Leeds University coach was an old fighter, a former profes-sional called Mike Sunderland, and he was to become a good friend. On that first evening I sparred with a clumsy cruiserweight and a slightly less ineffectual middleweight. It was difficult to avoid hurting them.

Afterwards Mike said, 'You've done a bit, haven't you. Let's get you on the scales. You'll do nicely against Cambridge.'

My enforced dieting had brought my weight down to under eleven stone.

Mike said, 'That's awkward. We've got a fair middleweight. He's got a chance, but we want a cruiserweight. You reckon you could fight light-heavy?'

I said doubtfully, 'I'd be giving away about a stone and a half.'

He grinned. 'In this class you could take on six cruisers at once. What about it?'

I agreed and when the training session was over we went to a pub where we met another old fighter, Tom Mallison, who had fought world class men in England and the United States during the years following the First World War. They were both scarred, craggy old men, survivors of the days when you fought fifteen three-minute rounds for a fiver out of which you paid your manager's cut and your own expenses, yet they were both immensely kind, rather sentimental, simple and gentle.

I won all my fights at Leeds and I collected the Northern Universities Championships at welter, middle and cruiserweight. Mike also fixed me up with more exacting contests at A.B.A. tournaments in Huddersfield and Bradford and he would wangle generous expenses and arrange for me to sell my silver cup or canteen of cutlery back to the suppliers at a discount, so I was able to make a little money.

It was through my boxing that I infiltrated into another sector of Leeds society, one that I would probably have been wiser to avoid. I was in the alley pub in Briggate one evening when the barmaid placed a fresh pint of bitter in front of me and said, 'From the gents over there.' She nodded towards two strangers who were watching me with encouraging smiles.

I raised the pint in salute and drank and they returned the salute with their own glasses. The younger of the two looked to be in his late twenties or early thirties and he had a flattened nose and cauliflower ear. His companion was about forty, very snappily dressed in the fashion of the time and place, jaunty felt-hat, well-padded shoulders, fingers flashing with huge rings.

The one who looked like a boxer came over to where I was

standing and said, 'Come and have a chat. My friend'd like to talk to you. He's a useful bloke to know.'

The older man was called Sam and the younger, Teddy. Teddy was not, it appeared, a boxer but he had been until recently a fairly successful all-in wrestler. He had appeared in the ring under the name of The College Boy because, as he explained with complacency, unlike most of his profession he was good-looking and well-educated, by which I understood him to mean that he could read and write and that his features, though mis-shapen, were still recognizably human.

'Saw you fight,' Sam said. 'Huddersfield Town Hall against that Liverpool boy. You could go a long way. That right, Teddy?'

'That's right.'

'You ever think of turning pro?'

I said, 'Not really.'

'You could make a bit of brass. Why fight for tin cups and fish knives when you can get paid for it?'

I said I would think it over.

After that first meeting I often had a drink with Sam and Teddy and through them I met other raffish characters who appeared to exist at varying levels of prosperity without following any profession or regular employment. One of them was another ex-boxer named Benny who was usually accompanied by two or three thuggish-looking henchmen who would say little but stand by watchfully like dangerous hounds, devoted speechlessly to their master and highly menacing to anything that seemed to threaten his safety. Benny himself was quite different: a fastidiously neat dresser, his face was smooth, pink and plump and his little dark eyes were bright, his mouth small and red, his dark hair lustrous and always perfectly barbered. He looked almost doll-like, a dapper and pretty little gentleman, until you got close and noticed that one ear was bunched like a small fist and through the dark hair of his eyebrows the scar-tissue gleamed like silver.

I do not know what class of boxer he had been. At this time he was busy with various criminal activities and was shortly to be arrested for robbery with violence, but I found him agreeable and amusing, even witty in the staccato sniping manner of the back street, the gym, race-track and sporting saloon bar. Certainly, when he was around, I was always sure of free drinks which were bestowed with the kind of panache with which great lords once threw money to their retainers.

One of his acquaintances, a big fleshy man named Lee who, like Teddy, had once been a wrestler, was also very kind-hearted and one bitterly cold day he remarked that I had no overcoat. He took me to his room, which was not far from where I lived in Chapeltown, and presented me with an old one. It had been tailored at a time when it had been fashionable in Lee's circle to wear top-coats of great length with enormous padded shoulders, vast lapels and exaggerated waists. On me this coat almost swept the ground and the shoulders, designed for a heavyweight wrestler of seventeen stone, drooped wearily on my comparatively slight frame. I must have looked odd, swathed from chin to toe in faded black melton, but the thing kept out the cold and I was grateful for it.

I moved then from one territory to another, not fully at home in either yet happy to take from each what I found valuable. The kindness, the toughness and seedy glamour of Lee and Benny and their circle could sometimes draw me away from the more austere pleasures offered by the company of my friends at the University and the solitude of my room in Francis Street, but I was always glad to get back, refreshed, to the reading and the talk of literature.

The knowledge that my freedom must sooner or later be snatched from me informed in some way every moment and, though it caused me anxiety and distress, it also charged my life with a value and intensity that it has since only occasionally been able to contain. And when, in the summer of 1947, the law finally caught up with me it was obvious from my reaction that I had been preparing myself subconsciously for this experience.

My arrest occurred on a Sunday afternoon when I was sitting in my room reading, of all things, *Crime and Punishment*. There was a sudden banging of heavy feet on the stairs and the next moment my door burst open and two men in plain clothes charged into the room, grabbed me and pulled me to my feet.

'All right,' said one of them. 'We're police officers. We know all about you.'

The other officer let go of me and began to prowl around the room, picking up books and papers, peering suspiciously into nooks and crannies. I felt curiously unalarmed and when, a little while later in the thoughtful quiet of the cells, I had time to analyse this feeling I realized that, after the first instinctive shock, there was a strong undercurrent of relief in my sense of resignation.

'What's your name?' said the detective who still held me.

I told him my name and I was taken out to their car and driven to the Central Police Station where, although I admitted I was a deserter from the Army and gave them the name of my unit, I was still interrogated for some time since the detectives were reluctant to believe that I had not been engaged in criminal activities of some kind. Everybody knew, they said, that deserters couldn't get jobs so they had to take up villainy. It stood to reason. They even tried, with elephantine clumsiness, to trap me into confessions of misconduct and it would have been tempting to tease them a little except that they were both very large men of uncertain temper.

When at last they gave up questioning me, I was locked in a cell with lavatorial tiled walls and a wooden bunk and three grimy-looking blankets. I would be taken up before the magistrate the next morning for the formality of being remanded for military escort and then I would have to wait for a couple of days or so until the Gordon Highlanders sent an N.C.O. and two other-ranks, suitably armed, to take me back to face trial by court martial. I had been on the run for two years and two months and was likely to get a heavy sentence. It was cold in the cell and summer and my precarious liberty seemed far away. I never did discover who, if anyone, put the police on to my track, and I have never felt much interest in the matter.

NOW

OVER a month has passed since I began writing this, and I dare not look over what I have so far set down for fear that I should find my evocations of past incidents and people so pale and lifeless that I shall be discouraged from continuing. Beyond my window, Tom Payne's Hill is festering with half-thawed, grey snow, and the sky is like the lining of a great coffin.

I have just returned from Liverpool where I have been reading poetry to audiences in schools and colleges and—on one rather less formal occasion—in a pub where I was joined by the very amiable Adrian Henri and Roger McGeogh. 'Pop Poetry' is not for me. It seems to bear less relation to real poetry than a fixed fight does to a genuine one. It is an amateurish branch of the entertainment industry and the verses are, at best, whimsical or weakly flip and otherwise grossly self-indulgent, formally sloppy, ill-written, sentimental as sugar love-hearts and disposable as paper knickers. They make use of the stock language of the ad-man to produce the copywriter's stock images which evoke stock responses from an audience to whose intelligence, imagination and feelings no challenge whatsoever is made.

I am glad to be back in Dorset to the monochrome but sustaining routine of life here, to the children, my books, my work, the more or less regular meals, the pub, the daily postal delivery which might one day contain the magic envelope, the enormous legacy or the offer that will bring me vast wealth and reputation, to the radio and the newspapers which I never find time to do more than glance through. Today's *Times*, I see, carries a report of the Frazier–Ellis World Heavyweight title fight. Frazier won easily when Ellis, after taking a hammering, failed to come up for the fifth round. The same old story: the nice guy, the stylish boxer, bulldozed into ignominious defeat by the brute strength of the scowling slugger.

Boxing still fascinates me, though less so than once it did. I am getting a bit squeamish now and I have not actually been to a show since my last visit to the A.B.A. Finals three years ago when I found that I was wincing when a boy walked into a really big punch. I would not prevent my sons from taking up the game but I know that I would not be able to watch them in the ring. Certainly I would be sorry to see boxing outlawed. Even now I find that the great heroes of the game possess a mythopœic power and stature that no other type of athlete can claim: there was Jack Johnson, menacing, insolent and incomparable; Battling Siki who walked the streets with a pet leopard on a leash and died in Hell's Kitchen with a knife in his back; Dempsey and Tunney, the savage puncher and the icy perfectionist; Jimmy Wilde, 'the ghost with the hammer in his hand', who weighed no more than seven stone yet could hit with the power of a man twice his size. There was Georges Carpentier, the handsome Frenchman who fought with the grace and ferocity of a panther and knocked out our Joe Beckett in less time than it takes to tie one shoe; there was Tony Galento, the Boston Beer Barrel, a Falstaff of a fighter who trained on a diet of beer and cigars and hired superannuated pugs to do his road-runs for him while he followed them in the back of a limousine—yet he put the legendary Joe Louis on the canvas before he himself was knocked out. A roll-call of the great champions can still stir me like a rough heroic poem.

I have never subscribed to the commanding officer or headmaster belief that 'boxing makes a man of you', that it gives courage to the timid, bouncing self-confidence to the shy and changes the sneak and cad into an honest good sport. As a moral therapy I should say that it is a dead loss. But what it can do—and here it is like art—is give a man a chance to behave in a way that is beyond and above his normal capacity. The great artist may be, outside the confines of his art, cruel, weak, arrogant and foolish, but within them he can transcend his own condition and become noble, passionate and truthful beyond the range of ordinary men. Something similar happens with the great fighter, too. He may be stupid, vain, ignorant and brutish—though he is not, in fact, these things nearly

48

as often as popular belief imagines—but in the exercise of his art he becomes the embodiment of transcendental courage, strength and chivalry. I have seen it happen and I have experienced the Aristotelean catharsis as powerfully in the boxing stadium as in the theatre.

There are other parallels between the roles of the artist and the fighter. The good boxer, like the good artist, must have mastered all the basic orthodox techniques, but he must also be inventive and resourceful enough to adapt and modify these as new and un-expected problems are set before him; the boxing contest, like the poet's, painter's or composer's struggle with his medium, must be conducted within the limits of strict rules; both the artist and the fighter must be dedicated to their tasks, they must both submit to the arduous preparation for the encounter, they must both exercise the same watchfulness in action, and neither must play to the gallery.

Of course it is a dangerous sport, but no more so than many others, and the risk of injury, even fatal injury, must be present. All the protests against the brutality of the game and the exploitation of the boxers never come from the fighters themselves because they know, at some level of consciousness, that if the dangers of the sport were removed the whole thing would become meaningless. The dangers dignify the game; without them there would be no oppor-tunity to show heroic courage, generosity in defeat and triumph, and supernatural strength. To ask that the boxer should be padded and protected from injury seems as absurd to the fighter as asking the big-game hunter to go on safari with blank ammunition in search of stuffed lions.

Yet, as I said, as I grow older I become more squeamish. I would hate to see a boy hurt in the ring and, if that boy were my own son, it would be intolerable. But I believe that he must be given the right to choose whether or not to risk being hurt. I chose to take the risk myself and I have never regretted it. I am much less sure about most of my other choices.

THEN

MY ESCORT arrived at the police station after five miserable days and I was taken, wearing handcuffs, on the long train journey to Aberdeen where, in the Brig o' Don Barracks stores, my civilian clothes were taken away and I was put back into uniform. Going into the guard-room was like the resumption of an old and disgusting habit. I was put in a cell with two other prisoners, one a man of about thirty who, although he was awaiting trial as a deserter, claimed that he had never been in the Army at all and that his call-up papers had arrived while he had been at sea with the Merchant Navy in which he had served throughout the war. He was a fairly intelligent man who carried with him that indefinable but unmistakable air of un- reliability and falsehood that most con men communicate. Every- thing he said was plausible and put across with an excess of candour that immediately kindled suspicion. The other was a big, gingery Highlander with a red face and hot, aggrieved little eyes. He had been with the Gordons all through the war and had been demobbed from Germany where he had served in the Army of Occupation. Civilian life with a wife and two children had not proved to his taste and he had re-enlisted, expecting to be returned to the paradise of post-war Germany where, as he assured us, you could get a young *Fräulein* for a handful of fags or a tin of bully and you could make an easy fortune on the black market. But the Army had played a dirty trick on him and posted him to the depot in Aberdeen, only a few miles from his home in Banff. So he had gone on the run and had been picked up in Glasgow after only a few weeks of liberty.

As prisoners awaiting trial we were not obliged to do any work other than scrubbing out the cell and keeping it tidy, so the days were long and tedious. The Regimental Police seemed very young and much less formidable than those I remembered from my recruit days. The Orderly Officer, who visited the cell on his daily tour of duty, also seemed very young, a pink-faced boy playing at soldiers. I was twenty-five years old; seven years had passed since my enlistment and I felt my age as both burden and armour.

I was taken before the Commanding Officer of the depot and remanded for a court martial. In the cell I played draughts with the former merchant seaman on an improvised board and read old newspapers, magazines and the few thrillers that the more friendly R.P.s would occasionally throw in to us. Nights were the worst times: sleep did not come easily and the sense of isolation from the free world was strongest then. I would lie and think about my friends in Leeds, about my books and papers in the room in Francis Street and I would try not to worry too much about my impending court martial.

A young subaltern was given the job of acting as my defending officer. He came to see me in the cell and the other two prisoners were taken elsewhere so that we could confer in privacy.

He said, 'If you've any objection to my defending you, you can say so and they'll detail someone else.'

I said I had no objection.

He was rather embarrassed and not sure what manner to adopt.

'I suppose you'll plead guilty. Well, I mean, you could hardly plead anything else.'

'Hardly,' I said.

'Well, the only thing we can do is try and plead mitigating circumstances. Point is, you deserted after hostilities were over. I gather you'd done your bit satisfactorily. Got wounded, that sort of thing. That should help a bit. Perhaps—no offence, you understand— perhaps we might suggest you were a bit—not bomb-happy exactly—but something like that. Nerves playing you up. Not sleeping well. That sort of thing. What do you think?'

I said that it sounded worth a try.

'Oh, and by the way, you can speak in your own defence if you like. I can ask the Court's permission for you to say your own piece. That is, if you feel it would do any good.'

I doubted whether it would do any good but I thought I ought to say my piece.

'Yes, all right.' He hesitated, half turned away to leave and then seemed to change his mind. 'Er, by the way, what *were* your reasons? Off the record. I mean honestly, why *did* you get off your mark? After all you'd have been demobbed if you'd waited for a few months. You'd have got your gratuity money and all the rest of it.'

I said, 'If I hadn't gone when I did, I'd have gone crazy. I'd had enough. That's all.'

He nodded vaguely, his eyes glazing slightly. 'Er, yes . . . I see. Ah well, nothing else? Oh by the way, I'll tell the Provost Sergeant to get your battledress blouse into the tailors. You'll have to wear your ribbons for the Court. I'll let you know the date as soon as it's fixed. Shouldn't be long now.'

He left, my cell-mates returned and we discussed our forthcoming trials, played draughts for a while and later, in the sad and randy twilight, we talked of bints and booze-ups and getting back to civvy street. It was disturbing to find how quickly one settled back into the army mould. The rough khaki no longer prickled and itched and the great leather boots no longer weighed heavily on the feet. My hair had been cropped and I hardly noticed that the mechanical obscenities of the barrack-room had crept back into my speech. And yet there was a difference: I was conscious of being someone other than the person who had walked out of Hamilton Barracks two years earlier and at least part of my apparent reversion to type was an act performed to make life in the guardroom easier both for my companions and myself.

I wrote letters to George Wilson Knight and Bonamy Dobrée, both of whom volunteered to speak or write on my behalf to the President of the court martial and they and other Leeds friends sent me a variety of books which, as an untried prisoner, I was allowed to receive. I began to rehearse in my mind the speech I would make to the court martial: I would simply tell the truth. I would explain that I had reached the point in 1945 when I had to get out of the Army or be finished off as a human being. I had enlisted for the duration of hostilities and once the war in Europe came to an end I was justified in releasing myself. I would speak briefly, with directness and clarity, and let them make of it what they could.

The reality, of course, was a lot different from the fantasies in which I had performed my part with dignity and the calm resolution of the morally unassailable. I was marched into the court martial room in a manner that was anything but dignified and my heart was clenched and thumping like a heavy fist. The President of the Court was a middle-aged major of the Pioneers, but the younger members, a moustached Black Watch captain and a Seaforth Highlander, looked keen, fierce, and, when their regard came my way, contemptuously disapproving.

The Prosecuting Officer merely read out the dates of my desertion and arrest and quoted statements made by the policemen who had picked me up. My Defending Officer was clearly nervous and anxious to get his performance over as quickly as possible. He said that here was a man whose desertion was not denied, indeed could not be denied, but his act, while to be deplored, had not been that of a coward and the Court might take into consideration, when passing sentence the fact that the accused had seen a good deal of action and had acquitted himself quite satisfactorily under fire. He had fought in the Middle East and in Normandy where he had received gunshot wounds in both legs and was probably at the end of his nervous tether when he had gone absent from his unit. Would the Court permit the accused to speak for himself and explain his own reasons for his desertion? The Court conferred and the President nodded. I was invited to speak.

I had hoped to sound adult, intelligent and manly, without either vanity or excessive humility, but something happened to my vocal chords and the voice that issued from my mouth was unfamiliar to my own ears, unfamiliar and unpleasant, a quavering and rather plaintive treble. I said that I had spent almost five years in the Army and I had found the life, both in and out of action, totally destructive of the human qualities I most valued, the qualities of imagination, originality, sensitivity and intelligence. I had felt whatever traces of these qualities I might possess being steadily destroyed and I knew, in May 1945, that I would either have to surrender to the extinction of my humanity or escape from the military life. I believed that I might be a writer but I would never get the chance to find out unless I got away before it was too late. While I regretted any trouble I had caused the military and civilian authorities, I still believed that my action had been the only one I could have sensibly taken.

I must have sounded unbelievably priggish and self-pitying and my breathless and squeaky delivery could not have helped my cause very much.

My judges conferred again. Then the President said, 'You say you want to be a writer? What kind of thing do you write?'

'Poetry,' I said.

Significant looks were exchanged by the Board. The Seaforth smirked and the Black Watch officer looked grim. The President looked worried.

A few moments later I was marched out of the room where I waited with my escort for about twenty minutes, during which I cursed myself for my feeble performance. Then the Regimental Sergeant-major was summoned before the President and he reappeared a few seconds later and said to the Provost-Sergeant: 'He's remanded for a psychiatrist's report. Take him back to the digger.'

I was marched back to the guardroom and locked up in the cell.

'How did it go?' said the merchant seaman.

I told him I was remanded for a psychiatrist's report.

The Highlander was envious. 'You lucky bastard,' he said. 'Them trick-cyclists are all nut-cases themselves. You'll get your ticket for sure. You see if you don't.'

*

Ten days later I was escorted to Maryhill Barracks in Glasgow for my examination by the Army psychiatrist. I had flirted with the idea of parading alarming symptoms of mental disorder but common sense warned me that I would be unlikely to deceive a man who had probably seen through the pretences of scores of more skilled malingerers, so I gave up any idea of preparing myself for the interview and decided to play my part by ear. Since the court martial I had not been sleeping well, assailed by alternate hopes and doubts about the outcome of this meeting, and by the time I was led into the psychiatrist's office I was in a state of half-somnolent resignation.

My escort was dismissed and I was told to sit down facing the psychiatrist across his desk. He was a major in the Medical Corps and I was not reassured by his manner, which was brisk and impersonal, or by his face which was impassive, his eyes guarded yet vigilant behind thick-lensed spectacles.

He questioned me for about half an hour about my reasons for desertion, my childhood relationships with my parents, my sexual experiences and ambitions, my religious and political beliefs and the state of my physical health.

Then he said, 'You're trying to avoid punishment, aren't you? You're hoping to keep out of gaol.'

I had found him unsympathetic from the start, if not actually hostile, and I was annoyed as much by the truth of what he said as by its unfairness.

I said irritably, 'I didn't ask to be sent here. I've never said I was sick. I'm here because I was brought here. Don't blame me if you've been wasting your time. Blame the people who sent me.'

He seemed unmoved by my show of exasperation. 'Then you don't think there's anything the matter with you?'

'No.'

He smiled faintly and ambiguously. 'How do you think you'd stand up to a long sentence?'

'I expect I'd survive.'

'Yes, I expect you would.'

He seemed to lose interest in me and he leaned back in his chair, eyes fixed on the ceiling. I could hear the recruits being drilled on the square below the window, the crunch of boots and the bellowings of an N.C.O.: 'Ef-ight, ef-ight, up-ight, swing . . . them . . . arms, up-'ight, ef-ight . . . Squad . . . halt.'

The major brought his gaze back to me.

'There are many men serving sentences who're in a lot worse shape than you,' he said.

I did not reply.

He went to the door and called my escort into the room.

'All right, that's all. You can take him away,' he said.

*

Back in the guardroom I waited for the results of the examination to reach Aberdeen. I knew what would then happen. The report

55

would say that I was perfectly fit to receive punishment, I would be hauled up for sentence, there would be a wait of a few days until the findings of the court martial were confirmed by the general commanding the district and then I would be sent either to a detention barracks or, if I were dishonourably discharged and given hard labour, to a civilian prison.

The merchant seaman was suddenly ordered to pack his kit and was taken away to a mysterious destination; two rumours later circulated, the first more plausible than the second: one, that he had been returned to Peterhead Gaol from which he had not long before escaped and the other that he had been identified as a former German agent and was being interrogated by M.I.5. His place was taken by a stocky Glaswegian called Hughie MacIver, a regular detention-wallah who had served more time in the glasshouse than he had with his unit.

Hughie was very proud of his wide experience of various detention barracks and he claimed that he had done more time inside than any other soldier with his length of service in the British Army. He claimed particular credit for having skipped all of eight attempts to get him overseas and his finest single achievement was when they took him, firmly handcuffed, straight from the guardroom on to the troopship.

'They thought they'd got me that time,' he said. 'They wouldna take off the cuffs till they'd got me on the big boat at Greenock. Rommel must a been aye worried when he heard I was on my way. I was a wee bit worried myself. But as soon as it got dark I was over the side like a flash and I had a mile's swim to the shore. I was kipping up with a lassie no far away and you should have seen her face when I came round. Just my vest and pants on, freezing to death. Seven months it was before they caught up with me and they wouldn't have got me then but I went and got drunk. A good job I had, too, lifting the coal.'

He told me that I would probably get two years.

'You'd be better getting civvy nick. It's dead cushy. Detention's a proper bastard. Everything at the double. Packdrill at the double, every time you move, you move at the double, no matter what you're on. You even go for a shit at the double. No fags, terrible grub. The

56

Staff, they'll do you as soon as look at you. I'm not kidding. You get P.D. One for fuck all. That's bread and water and solitary. Civvy nick's a doddle at the side of Detention. It's like a rest cure.'

The light faded in the cell and Hughie's voice went on, lugubrious, sourly mocking and irrepressible. Outside, the bugle sounded Lights Out, sweet and hoarse in the summer night. I lay between the blankets waiting for the short reprieve of sleep. Hughie began to talk of the last girl he had had in Cambuslang.

'She's a wee darling. Classy too. She's educated. Not one o' they brass nails. She works in an office. I'm telling you, she's a wee smasher. She'd give me anything she would. She kept me in fags and she'd always slip me a couple of pound for a dram. Aye, she was a beaut. And what a ride! She really loved it, couldn't get enough. Squealed like a wee pig she did.' There was a pause. 'And I suppose some lucky bastard'll be getting across her the now. Och well, that's the way it goes.'

He began to sing in a nasal bar-room voice a song called *You are my Sunshine*. Half-way through his first encore there was a loud banging on the cell door and a voice shouted, 'Cut it out in there! Stop that bloody row and get to kip.'

'Cut it out yourself, you tartan-faced whore!' Hughie shouted back, but he stopped singing and before long I heard his breathing compose itself to the regular measure of sleep. But it was a long time before I slept.

*

Three days later, shortly after breakfast, the cell door opened and an R.P. yelled, 'Stand by your beds!'

The Provost-Sergeant came in.

'Right, you,' he said, pointing to me. 'Get your small kit packed. The word just came through. You're away to Birmingham at 0950 hours. Northfield Hospital.'

He strutted out and the cell door was bolted behind him.

For a few seconds I could not take in the good news.

Then Hughie said, 'Jesus Christ! You've done it! You've worked a flanker. Northfield, that's the nutters joint! You'll get your ticket.

Holy Christ, some people get the luck. You'll be in civvy street inside a couple of months.'

I could not believe my luck and even when, again under escort, I was on my way to Birmingham, I still felt that a mistake had been made which would be discovered and rectified with my being hauled back to Aberdeen and then sent to my proper destination, a detention barracks or civil prison. But no mistake had been made: that apparently unsympathetic major at Maryhill Barracks had either taken pity on me or he had really believed that I was mentally sick.

When I was delivered at Northfield I was put in a closed ward, that is a ward that was kept locked and where the patients were always under careful supervision, for they were either potentially dangerous to themselves or others or, like myself, they were considered too unreliable to be kept in an open ward from which it would be easy to escape. The other patients were a mixed lot. Some had attempted suicide; there were manic depressives and a case of hysterical amnesia, a couple of epileptics and a number of hunted-looking men who prowled restlessly about, speaking to no one. To form a friendship, or even make the most superficial contact, with anyone here presented problems that would not be encountered in an ordinary hospital, for almost everyone was imprisoned in the mesh of his own obsessions, fears and anxieties. There was something, too, in the very atmosphere of the ward, something enervating and depressing like a non-olfactory stink, a bad smell in the head, as if the air had been infected by the collective melancholy and morbidity of the men who lived in it.

There was only one patient at Northfield with whom I was able to communicate: he was a few years older than I and had been called up early in the war, had deserted after a few days in uniform and had continued to desert at every opportunity. His interludes of liberty were always brief because he always went straight home to his wife and stayed there, and while he did his best to hide from the police when they called it was never long before they caught him. If an almost obsessive uxoriousness can be classified as a neurosis, then he was neurotic, but in all other respects he seemed fairly well-balanced and he might reasonably have argued that successful adjustment to a destructive and dehumanizing environment such as the military life was a sign of a predisposition to mental sickness rather than health.

He was a gentle, good-humoured cockney. His love and longing for his wife were not the consequence of a jealous anxiety to be with her in case a rival should usurp his place: as far as I could tell, the possibility never occurred to him. She was quite simply the pivot of his existence, his sole reason for being, and every moment spent away from her was a moment squandered. This circumstance made him a rather boring companion because, whatever we might be talking about, he would soon manage to work an opening into the conversation that would admit a prolonged eulogy on the beauty, goodness and loyalty of his wife.

The physical conditions of life in the hospital should have provided me with a fine opportunity to read and write, but that sour air, the feeling of squirming fears, delusions, and sick torments that were being endured all around me, the occasional outbursts of hysterical violence and the claustrophobia, all made sustained concentration impossible. I read Walton's lives of Donne and Herbert and I got about half-way through *The Prelude* but otherwise I read nothing but thrillers and I wrote nothing at all.

The psychiatrist in charge of the ward was a young captain, overworked and sceptical about the value of anything that could be done for his patients at Northfield. I was briefly interviewed by him on my second day at the hospital but I did not see him again for almost a fortnight, during which I was beginning to feel that I would rot in the closed ward for months or even years and that the more strenuous miseries of the glasshouse might after all have been preferable. Then the psychiatrist sent for me again.

He said, 'I'm sorry I've not been able to see you before but I've been run off my feet. Well, I've got good news for you. I've arranged for you to have a Medical Board. It'll take time, probably a few weeks, so for goodness' sake don't get impatient and do anything silly. The point is, we want to get you out of here. If you are ill— and I don't think you are—then this is the last place to get well. I can't see going to prison would do you or anybody else any good. So a Board is the thing. Perhaps I shouldn't tell you this, but I will.

It'll be a pure formality. You'll be discharged, you can take my word for it. So thank your lucky stars and for God's sake keep your nose clean in the meantime.'

My first feelings were of wild exhilaration and almost unbearable excitement but when the fever of joy subsided I was troubled by an unease, a curious melancholy and self-distaste that I recognized as guilt. The shades of all those men who had done nothing worse than I and were now serving long prison sentences rose to accuse me. But they were not my only accusers. I had survived a war in which many men, some of them my friends, and all with as much to live for as I, had been killed; they lay in the sands of Libya or in the orchards and meadows of Normandy and, however clean they kept their noses, no Board would give them their discharge. They, too, accused, and they accuse me still. Pity for the dead is a wasted emotion, or so my reason tells me, but the heart is deaf to such counsel and it grieves for those young lives brutally and prematurely ended, and the grief is poisoned with guilt and an obscure fear that in some way and at some time full payment for one's outrageous good fortune will be exacted.

NOW

THE first days of summer have come at last and I would find this golden afternoon somnolent except for the shrieks of pain, wrath and derision of my warring children who are making the garden into a little battlefield. I leave them to it. If you can't lick 'em, don't join 'em. The bigger they are, the harder I fall. I try to close my ears to the noise and go on writing this.

I suppose I am a pretty ineffectual father in most positive ways, but I console myself that at least I am not often intolerant or repressive, and, whatever errors of omission I may be guilty of, I shall not be remembered by my children as an ogre and, if their adult recollections of childhood are not happy, I trust that it will not be my shade which casts the darkness over them.

I am sure that the experience of childhood during the past half-century in England differs very little essentially from generation to generation and from one environment to another. There are still, of course, wretchedly unhappy childhoods of almost unrelieved misery, where the child is the victim of thoughtless or deliberate cruelty, but such a childhood is at least as likely to occur in a middle or upper class environment as in any other, even the poorest, and is as likely to be experienced today as it was, say, thirty or forty years ago. We have all read nostalgic accounts of picnics on the lawns of gracious country houses, of little Christopher or Nigel delightedly receiving his first pony, new cricket bat or bicycle; we have enjoyed affectionate portraits of loving nanny or gruffly protective gardener or groom, descriptions of a Christmas expedition to the theatre and the great shops of the city and returning in the Daimler to hot buttered muffins in the nursery, memories of the sadness of departing for prep school, a sadness quickly subsumed by the excitement of new friendships, challenges and adventures. But for obvious reasons—

lack of the leisure rather than lack of literacy being one of the main ones—we have read a good deal less of young Alf or Fred, his memories of the visiting uncle giving him coppers to spend, the fried chips under the street lamplight, the races with rusty, spoke-less cycle rims for hoops, the thrill of the maiden voyage on the trolley made by Dad from the chassis of an old pram, the pleasures of waiting outside the pub at Sunday dinner-time and hearing the tobacco-stained voices rumbling inside and smelling the pungent whiffs of malt and shag and savouring fizzy lemonade and potato crisps in the warm sunlight; we do not often read of battles fought with improvised wooden swords and guns on derelict plots or building sites, but, despite the superficial differences of background and apparatus, the pleasures experienced by all children are very similar in quality and intensity.

It is the same with the miseries: a slap over the lug from Mum or a couple of licks of Dad's belt cause no greater distress than Mummy's tearful reproaches or Daddy's stern reprimand and, in any case, the dolours of children seem much more the consequence of temperamental predisposition than the treatment meted out by those in authority. One has only to watch one's own children to feel serious doubts about the effects of environment on personality and behaviour, for here are my five, all brought up in the same style and the same kind of home, yet all quite different in character, tastes, temper and aspirations.

Much of my own unhappiness as a child proceeded, I suspect, from a temperamental leaning towards melancholy and a great capacity for being bored that might have been exacerbated by neglect and the wrong kind of attention but were not caused by them. I see something of this, though only a little, in my ten-year-old son, Toby, who will flop in a chair and groan aloud with sheer ennui and seem totally unable, physically or mentally, to drag himself from his dark and suffocating inertia, yet at other times, when his interest has been engaged, can occupy himself busily and happily for hours on end with some private game. Though he is usually quite sociable he is not a gregarious child and his pleasures tend to be lonely ones. I doubt whether he will ever voluntarily play for any kind of athletic team but I can imagine him enjoying the more solitary activities of exploration, long walks, camping and climbing.

None of my children has so far shown special enthusiasm for literature though it is true that my daughters, aged thirteen and fifteen, both read a good deal of fiction, but at the mention of poetry they will blench and pull the kind of face that is usually provoked by the offer of tapioca pudding. Of course I would not dream of trying to persuade them to read poetry while they are convinced that it has nothing to offer them, but I do hope that their prejudice will be overcome by some person or circumstance so that they will not be deprived for ever of one of the most enriching of human experiences.

In my own childhood, reading was a way of escape from those terrible onslaughts of boredom and dissatisfaction with ordinary existence and I was a fluent and avid reader from the age of six, though I did not read poetry with any pleasure until I was about thirteen and then only one or two poems that I had happened to come across in the dreadful school anthology whose main function was the punitive one of providing the teachers with a useful source of written impositions. My discovery of the Methuen anthology came later when I was fifteen and had left school and was browsing in a second-hand bookshop where I picked it up and opened it at the de la Mare poem which begins:

> When I lie where shades of darkness
> Shall no more assail mine eyes,
> Nor the rain make lamentation
> When the wind sighs;
> How will fare the world whose wonder
> Was the very proof of me?
> Memory fades, must the remembered
> Perishing be?

I was instantly and permanently hooked.

Until then all my reading had demanded a narrative sufficiently compelling to draw me into its action and exclude the external world of reality; if I took any pleasure in the selection and manipulation of language, in its textures and cadences, it was purely accidental and largely unconscious, but now, for the first time, I could enjoy a kind of literature which, far from excluding the external world, illuminated it and in which the narrative or discursive element was of much less importance than the taste and feel, the strength and resonance of the words and their ordering and the strange power to haunt that certain images, lines and phrases possessed. I discovered then the truth of T. S. Eliot's comment, which I was not to come across until many years later, that poetry can communicate before it is understood.

But I am getting away from what I wanted to write about and that is the notion that almost everyone experiences very much the same childhood, however different its outward furnishings may be; and one can see one's own children living out situations which challenge or delight or torment them in almost exactly the same way that the onlooker was assailed so long ago and, through watching their present responses, is assailed again. Yet, with all the similarities, the shared hopes and fears, no two childhoods can be precisely alike and it is through the examination of those minute differences in experience and reaction that it might be possible to find out something, however little, about human personality and its astounding variety and sameness, its obstinate and paradoxical uniqueness.

One of the main problems with writing about your own childhood is the obvious one presented by the fallibility of memory and its way of remoulding the past to shapes determined by present needs. Those loving accounts of the author's early youth, dense with the minutiae of everyday living, may carry the feeling of truth, but it is closer to the truth of art than of life, for the author is using the selective and organizing powers of the creative artist rather than marshalling and recording the facts. No one can remember in detail the quotidian events of those very early days, so I shall not attempt a sustained narrative of childhood but instead sketch as accurately as I am able those events that have stayed, unchanged, in the memory for so long that they must be in some way relevant to what I am now.

THEN

OF BALLAGHADERREEN, where I lived between the ages of four and five, I remember only the main street and the convent, where I was taught by the Holy Sisters, and the little sweet shop and tobacconist in the back room of which my father had improvised a photographic studio and above which we lived, my parents, brother and I, in a couple of small rooms. Somewhere between home and the convent was a field with a pond into which I once fell or, far more likely, was pushed by my arch-enemy who darkened my days with fear and uncertainty, lying in wait for me on my return from school to beat me up with ruthless efficiency and jeer at my weakness, my tears and my English accent which, in the Ireland of 1926, was not likely to endear me to the natives. The name of my enemy was Bridie O'Shea and she frightened me more than anyone has frightened me since. I do not remember much about her appearance except that she was 'a big girl', that is to say she was a few years older than I and she was dark, hard and fierce like a gipsy. I still find it hard not to pull a face when I hear people talk of 'the weaker sex'.

Like almost everyone else in that time and place we were very poor and our food consisted mainly of soda-cake, potatoes and porridge with only occasional treats in the way of herrings, mutton stew or black pudding. In winter we burnt peat on the open fire and often, before bedtime, I would ask my mother to tell me about England, that Samarkand to which we would one day return, and she would repeat the unvarying account of the imaginary return journey—Irish train to Dublin, sea-voyage, English train to Beeston, and home to Chilwell Road where the best china would be brought out and we would have tinned peaches and marzipan-cake for tea. There were other stories that I liked to hear over and over again: one of these was about our neighbour, Martin Coffey, who

65

was cycling home one night from Sligo when he had to dismount to push his heavy old machine up a very steep hill. Suddenly he heard a strange voice, light and piping, coming from behind the hedge: 'Oh, Martin Coffey! Martin Coffey! Won't you come and dance with us?' The words were repeated two or three times in a lilting, sing-song rhythm. It was one of the little people inviting him to join in their nocturnal revel. But Martin was afraid that they would put a spell on him and entice him away to their own land from which he would never return to the world of human folk and—steep hill or not—he leapt on to his bicycle and pedalled furiously homeward with the sound of the little people's laughter gradually fading into the distance and the night.

In the summer we often had visits from tinkers who would come to the door with strings of mushrooms and, if you did not buy, they would put the evil eye on you. The female tinkers looked every bit as tough and wicked as the male, and the older ones always wore men's cloth caps and smoked blackened clay pipes that smelled a lot stronger than burning peat. They did not try to charm people into buying from them: their sales method was intimidation, but even their most menacing aspect and terrible maledictions were rarely effective against the invincible poverty that strangled charity, extravagance and often the fulfilment of elementary needs. I cannot imagine how the men got hold of enough money to drink on market days; perhaps they stole it or blackmailed the owners of illicit stills into supplying them with free potheen, but they often got drunk and fought viciously among themselves or against the more respectable common enemy until the civic guards arrived and clubbed them over the head and carted them off to the cooler.

I am not sure whether I actually saw any of these scenes of violence. I see them vividly enough now inside the head, but it is quite likely that these pictures were put there by my having heard grown-ups describing with retrospective relish those epic barneys. One thing I do remember with absolute clarity is a less violent but, to me, more important occurrence. I was walking alone down the main street one day when I saw, dumped in the gutter, the motionless body of a small mongrel dog. His lips were drawn back in a petrified and blackened snarl and the hairs around his mouth were stiff and spiked with congealed blood. He must have been a little dog because I quite easily picked him up and carried him home, to the horror of my mother who, when she had recovered from the shock, explained to me that he must have been kicked by a horse and that he was now dead and like all dead things he had to be buried.

I was very sorry for the dog but I felt no revulsion at all at the touch of his corpse or the sight of the blood that dripped from his mouth and spiked his beard, and I felt a protective tenderness that made me reluctant to hand him over to my father for burial. This little event was not imagined: its occurrence has been corroborated by my parents but my feelings might seem of doubtful authenticity. Yet I recall them, the very colour and flavour of them, so exactly that I believe my recollection to be genuine. It would be easy to explain my total lack of fear and repugnance by saying that I was too young to have any knowledge of the meaning of death, and later, when the sense of my own mortality had been thrust upon my consciousness, then I became squeamish and shrank from touching the bodies of dead creatures; but I am not at all sure that this is the whole explanation. As an adolescent I would have found it almost impossible to handle a dead animal: later, in manhood, the act would have demanded—and still, to some extent, demands—a conscious act of the will and the self-mocking reason, yet I do not think I am any more afraid of death, my own death, than many people who regularly handle cadavers, human or animal, without the slightest feeling of horror or disgust. I do not defend or justify my squeamishness; in fact I am ashamed of it and I feel inferior to those people who can kill and skin animals without a tremor of emotion, but I believe that this instinctive shrinking away from contact with the dead thing is a consequence of a fear, not so much of death, as its attendant corruption, and it seems possible that it was my ignorance or innocence of corruptibility that protected me from disgust and purified my pity for the dead mongrel that I brought in from the street. However irrationally or sentimentally, I value the memory of my dead dog as perhaps the sole reliable recollection I have of the state of innocence.

Yet I was not happy in Ireland; I recall little sunlight, much cold, darkness and drizzle; and my unhappiness was less to do with material poverty—which is only rarely a primary cause of childhood misery—than with a sense of alienation, a feeling of being different, of simply not belonging there. I can feel even now, almost half a century later, a faint reverberation from the joy and excitement that thrilled me when we at last decided to set off for England, but neither of the two images of the actual journey that I can confidently recapture is a particularly joyful one. The first is of my father thrusting on to my head a toddler's woolly bonnet with a pom-pom on the top and, to my indignant humiliation, being carried in his arms so that the ticket-clerk would think that I was under four years of age and therefore eligible to travel free of charge. The second image is the only surviving one of the voyage itself across the channel: a man was making his unsteady way below to the saloon and I was looking up, watching his descent. About half-way down he lost his footing and with a hoarse and wordless yell he tumbled to the bottom of the steps where his case burst open and something smashed and liquid that might have been urine or even blood spread over the floor. I thought he was badly injured since he needed the assistance of two or three men to get him to his feet, and even then he could not stand properly and was half-carried away out of my sight. The smell that came from the pool on the floor was neither piss nor blood; I would recognize it today without the least difficulty as Irish whiskey.

*

In Beeston we lived with my mother's parents in a small terrace house with an outside lavatory at the bottom of the little back garden. My brother and I slept together in one bed in the attic. I went to Nether Street Infants' School and in winter, to keep my hands warm, I would carry a baked potato which I would keep in my desk and eat at playtime. There was a sweet-shop near our house where you could buy tiny dried kernels that were called tiger nuts and tasted very sweet. The shop also stocked a delicacy that no one with whom I have since discussed the sweets of childhood seems to have come across: these were 'locusts', flat banana-shaped pods, dry and tough with a rather sinister flavour, like a cross between a prune and a date with a touch of furniture polish to ensure complete distinctiveness. I guess that these were the fruit of the carob tree, the locusts that were eaten by John the Baptist. Another unusual thing for a sweet-shop to sell was the tough and fibrous liquorice root, which you could go on chewing until it was a stringy, pulpy mess. Then there was a splendid assortment of more orthodox confectionery: black liquorice or spanish juice, aniseed balls, gobstoppers, sherbert-dabs, acid drops, spearmint, and one of my favourite indulgences in moments of affluence, a rich slab toffee embedded with nuts. The shop offered, too, a seductive ha'pennyworth called a 'sticky bag' which contained two or three ounces of mixed sweets that had for some reason deteriorated in quality, perhaps gone stale, melted in the sun or been damaged in transit. My brother and I were very properly forbidden by our parents to buy sticky bags but the temptation was too great and we would often sneak into the shop, put down our ha'pennies and hurry away to a quiet spot to devour our sickly purchases with guilty relish.

My grandfather was a slight, wispy man who wore spectacles with metal frames and smoked Woodbine cigarettes. I cannot remember ever seeing him light one or throw a finished one away. He always had a half-smoked cigarette drooping from his mouth. He was clever with his hands and he made wooden scooters for my brother and me; beautifully constructed and finished toys they were, far better than anything you could buy in a shop, and they gave us enormous pleasure and earned the envy of all our companions. For himself he built a wireless set and he would sit with the ear-phones on, chuckling at a comedian's patter while his wife, growing more and more angry at being excluded, nagged relentlessly at him: 'What are they saying? What's happening? Don't sit there giggling like a fool. Tell us what's going on. Give someone else a chance. I could smash that thing, I really could.'

On Sunday evenings my mother would play the piano and Grandfather the violin and then my father would sing to Mother's accompaniment, in a stern baritone, songs of great sentimentality with titles like *Tommy Lad* and *The Blind Ploughman*, and my brother and I would sit in the soft light of the gas mantles looking at the terrifying illustrations in a massive edition of *Pilgrim's Progress* or glancing through one of the volumes in Grandfather's set of *Popular Educators*, keeping very quiet in the hope that our presence would go unnoticed and we would be able to stay up beyond our usual bedtime.

Every Saturday afternoon my brother and I went to the children's matinée at the cinema. There were two picture palaces—as they were then called—in Beeston, and there was a good deal of rivalry between them for the patronage of the young Saturday afternoon audiences. The price of admission to each was twopence but one proprietor offered free sweets as an inducement to attend his show, and there, while the pianist vamped out popular tunes of the day, an usherette would come round distributing liquorice sticks or gob-stoppers, all of sticky-bag staleness since the stuff had been bought cheaply from the manager of a Nottingham confectioner who, in those lean days, could not sell his stock before quite a lot of it had lost its freshness.

The films were silent with captions at the foot of the screen and the ones we liked best were the cowboy pictures and the comedies. Tom Mix and Hoot Gibson were cowboy heroes and, of the funny men, I remember Charlie Chaplin, Buster Keaton, Ben Turpin and Harold Lloyd. Every week we were shown an episode from a serial and, at the end of each, the hero or the heroine would be left in a situation of appalling danger from which escape seemed quite impossible but, of course, was always accomplished at the beginning of the following week's episode.

There was something inexplicably disturbing about some of these early silent movies, a quality that I find hard to analyse or define and one that more recent films with their technical smoothness and more sophisticated content have almost certainly lost, a crude mythic power that the images of certain dreams possess, an ambiguity, a way of exciting half-recognized and conflicting emotions. A scene from one of the serial films, whose title and plot I have long forgotten, still returns when I invoke it as vividly as when I first saw it forty years ago: sailors mutinying, great bearded men, armed with belaying-pins, attack their officers who are well-laundered, clean-shaven, posh in their smart uniforms. The officers are desperately trying to remain calm, but their terror shows, they yield to it. They are violently manhandled, soon dishevelled and bruised, beaten and humiliated.

That scene was the archetype. There were others that excited me in the same way, violent confrontations between opposing types of men—pale-face and redskin, aristocrat and beggar, beauty and beast—and these scenes moved the imagination and a dormant sensuality in a curious way that I now realize was obliquely sexual. Perhaps prepubescent children today find the same kind of excitement in some television programmes and the experience which I relate to a particular place and time is a general one, but my own awareness of the first, subterranean tremors of pre-conscious sexuality is recalled with the sound of the strumming piano and the whiff of liquorice and chewing gum in the exciting darkness of the Beeston picture house.

It was about this time that I started to read the boys' twopenny weeklies—the 'tuppenny books' as we called them and were indignant to hear them miscalled 'comics', which were entirely different—*The Hotspur*, *The Skipper*, *The Wizard*, *The Rover* and *The Champion*. My taste for the fantasies of public school life, *The Magnet* and *The Gem*, came a little later when I felt the need for something a little more sophisticated than the crude legends of boys endowed with miraculous powers to make themselves invisible, of Klikibar, the warrior who subdued enemy tribes armed only with a cricket bat, of Cannonball Kelly the centre-forward who kicked the ball so hard that it carried three of the opposing defence with it into the net. And it was at this time, too, that I began to develop an almost obsessive interest in World War One.

The tuppenny books often contained free gifts and I think it was *The Champion* that gave away a little album and then, in subsequent weeks, photographs of the war to be stuck into the album, pictures of steel-helmeted men crouching below the sandbagged parapet of the trench, waiting to go over the top; pictures of shells exploding and throwing up huge black mushrooms of earth in the battered landscape of no-man's-land; pictures of gun-carriages, of stretcher-bearers struggling with their sad and patient burden through calf-deep mud, of tanks and broken churches, howitzers and Zeppelins, men blinded by poison gas, the barbed wire, the smashed trees, vistas of devastation, the shapes of unbearable terror, unbearable pain.

My father had served in France with The King's Own Scottish Borderers and he seemed to enjoy telling me tales of the trenches, and soon I became familiar with the furniture and language of the Tommy's war, with Jack Johnsons and whizz-bangs, Blighty-ones and Very-lights, duck-boards and dug-outs, and the names of the great battles sounded and echoed in my skull like a roll of drums or distant gunfire: The Somme, Loos, Passchendaele, Bapaume, Arras, Mons. I learnt the songs, too, those sad and jaunty tunes, sentimental or sardonic: *Mademoiselle from Armentières*, *Take Me back to Blighty*, *A Long Long Trail*, *Tipperary*, and *Pack up Your Troubles*. My father's accounts of his own experiences of war, even to my uncritical ear, soon began to sound implausibly heroic, and it was not long before I noticed that, in his re-tellings of a story, events and characters would change, the situations would become more dramatic and his own role more spectacular. I was not exactly bored by his tales but, in listening, I was able to block out the personal, self-aggrandizing parts and let only the poetry come through, the litany of proper names, the sacred objects, the landscape, the sadness, glory and waste.

I made a few friends in Beeston, the main one Teddy Smith, whose hair was very coarse and wiry and stuck up from his crown like the hair on a coco-nut and whose upper lip always gleamed with the snot that never stopped trickling from his snub nose. He was very scruffy and you could usually see his shirt tail sticking through the hole in the seat of his short trousers, and I was told to keep away from him because he probably had nits, if not something worse; but my parents' disapproval only strengthened my loyalty to him and we continued to play together.

We were sometimes accompanied by two brothers, Harry and Jess. Jess was much older than us—he was probably thirteen or fourteen—but he was severely retarded, and Harry, who was nine years old, had to assume responsibility for his elder brother. One of our favourite places to go in the summer was Bluebell Hill, a stretch of common land outside the town, and there, in a clearing at the centre of a small wood, pushing up through the long grass, was the roof of a house or large shed which had in some mysterious way sunk deep into the ground. The place frightened us: there was something unnerving about the notion of the building sinking into the earth as a waterlogged boat would be pulled down in a river, and I could not prevent my thoughts from pushing down into the dark underground interior and wondering what creatures lived in those strange rooms. It was frightening yet fascinating and we returned time after time, not going too close, watching the long bulk of the roof as if it were some kind of sleeping monster.

Another summer place to go was the River Trent where there was a gaiety of punts and skiffs and picnics, and you could hear all day long the tinny ragtime music played on portable gramophones drifting across the water from the brightly painted houseboats. But the benign appeal of the Trent was turned suddenly to menace when one day Jess and Harry were playing on their own near one of the deep locks and Jess fell into the greedy depths and Harry, his nine-year-old protector who could not swim a stroke, leapt in after him and both boys were drowned. After that, the river became for me an evil place and even on fine days, when it seemed to sparkle with good humour, I knew that it was dissembling, that its true nature was murderous and given its chance it would attack again.

This was the time of the Depression and work and money were both scarce. I am not sure what my father was doing for a living, nothing at all for longish periods, I suspect, though in the holiday season he would go to Skegness and work as a beach photographer. Grandfather was part-owner of a very small lace factory but the industry had been virtually strangled and he was finding it hard to keep going. Somehow enough cash was found for my father to take over a small photographic business in Derby, but it was decided that he would need the full-time help of my mother, so my brother stayed with my maternal grandparents and I was sent to my father's parents in Eccles, near Manchester.

*

Bardsley Street in Eccles, two facing rows of identical houses, little dark brick boxes, and at the top of the street a fence overlooking the reservoir, and behind the stretch of stagnant-looking water the dark mass of the sanatorium, the warehouse of sickness and pain and death. You went into my grandparents' house and found yourself in the front room, the parlour, which was used only for entertaining visitors. The family, my grandfather, grandmother and two uncles, lived in the kitchen, the only other downstairs room, where they ate, relaxed and washed and shaved at the cold water sink. Upstairs there were two bedrooms. My uncles, John and Percy, shared one, and I slept with my grandparents in the other. It smelled strongly of piss from the pot that they kept under their bed. The lavatory was outside in the little yard at the back of the house where there was also a small shed in which John kept his motor-cycle.

All the men in the family were employed, an unusual circumstance for those times. Grandfather and Percy worked for the Salford Council doing road repairs and John had a job at some kind of electrical plant at Barton. Both John and Percy were engaged to girls named Edith.

My paternal grandfather was a tall, grey-haired and handsome man whose nobility of features was enhanced rather than spoilt by his being totally blind in one eye and almost blind in the other. He seemed very old to me but he could not have been much past his mid-fifties. One of my jobs was to read the newspaper to him, chiefly the sporting news, and sometimes he would ask me to read aloud from whatever book I happened to be looking at, and he would listen with grave attention to the exploits of Sexton Blake, Harry Wharton and The Famous Five, Huckleberry Finn or David Balfour. Sometimes he was silent and withdrawn, locked away in the gathering darkness of his failing sight, and once or twice I saw him rise in anger to quell the defiance of one of his sons and, on these occasions, whichever uncle had invited the rebuke would be reduced to a sullen and rather frightened schoolboy. Yet Grandfather enjoyed moments of gaiety and he would often sit by the kitchen fire and sing comic songs or tell me stories about his boyhood, and quite often on Saturday afternoons he would take me on the tram to Salford where we would watch the local team play Rugby League Football though he could have seen little of what was going on in the field.

My grandmother was a plump, loving and lovable Lancashire woman who cooked magnificent meat and potato pie and was imperturbably good-natured. On Monday evenings, when her husband was out at a meeting of some mysterious society called, if I remember rightly, The Ancient Order of the Buffaloes, she would take me to the Regent Cinema where I saw my first 'talkies'. After the pictures we would buy fish and chips and Grannie would pick up a bottle of stout from the pub's off-sales and we would go home to our feast.

My memories of Eccles are mainly happy ones. This was the time when the cigarette manufacturers issued splendid cards showing brightly coloured pictures of railway locomotives, county cricketers, wildflowers, butterflies, aeroplanes, motor-cars and regimental badges, when Amy Johnson was a popular heroine whose praises were quite literally sung in a topical ditty called *Wonderful Amy* and Layton and Johnson sang irresistibly on Percy's tinny gramophone. The uncles did not, I think, have much in common except that they were both genial and unfailingly kind to me. John, the elder, was a great reader of tuppenny books and he regularly brought home *The Wizard*, *The Hotspur*, *The Union Jack* and *The Rover*. Percy was jovially contemptuous of John's reading habits, not because he considered the literature of his brother's choice to be inferior or childish, but because he considered any kind of reading—except for a glance at the newspapers—as a complete waste of time.

The only less than happy experiences that I can recall were unconnected with home. I had few friends and was vaguely aware of being different from the other children in Bardsley Street. This difference was partly to do with social rank and partly to do with temperament. In those days, particularly in urban society, the gradations of status within the working classes were numerous and often separated by little more than a hair's breadth. My mother was recognized by my father's family as being their social superior: her father was self-employed, she had been educated to the age of fifteen at a small fee-paying day school and she had been brought up as a lady to paint watercolours and to play the piano. Father had gone to a Board School, left at fourteen to work on the Manchester Ship Canal and he had joined the Army at the outbreak of war in 1914 to serve throughout in the ranks. His mother was a mill-girl who had left school at the age of twelve and his father had been an unskilled manual worker all his life. In marrying my mother, he had taken a

75

step up the social staircase and he was determined not to slip down again. So I had been brought up with a tacit belief in my superiority to rougher, more 'common' children, those whose fathers wore cloth caps and mufflers and whose mothers always seemed mountainous, slatternly, and much older than my own. Temperamentally I was not gregarious and adaptation to Bardsley Street juvenile society depended on acceptance by a gang rather than on the forming of individual friendships. I was not a gangable child. I preferred my own company or that of one or two others. I was viewed with suspicion and some hostility and regarded as stuck-up. There were three men working in our household and this meant that we were better off than most of our neighbours. The way I spoke invited derision. My accent was a weird hybrid, formed by Ireland and the English Midlands and, because I was an early and enthusiastic reader, my vocabulary was wider than is usual among children of eight. So I had to resign myself to being different, which meant being lonely.

I am not sure whether it was my accent, my 'difference', real or imagined, that caused my teacher at Clarendon Road Council School to dislike me so much. Perhaps it was something else, something more physical that excited in her impulses of sadism which she indulged through sarcasm, ear-tweaking and caning on the hands for reasons that seemed either non-existent or insufficient. She was a big woman with either blonde or white hair and a full moon of a face, pale, soft, and lightly powdered like uncooked pastry. She made my school life a misery and I used to lie in bed at night, planning the vengeance I would wreak when I grew up. We waged a long and merciless war but the advantages were all on her side. Sullen defiance did not stand much chance against the armoury that she could summon. I hated her with a passion that might have frightened her had she been aware of its intensity. She once made me cry, publicly and shamefully, yet it was not when she was being sarcastic or wielding her cane, but one day as she was patrolling the classroom while the children were writing their English compositions. I knew she was coming close to my desk and I prepared myself for some kind of attack. She stopped and looked down at my exercise-book for what seemed a very long time. I crouched, waiting for the blow to come down. Then, instead of the cuffed ear or the pincer-strong finger and thumb, she said, 'Well done. That's the best in the class by a long way.' Surprise, the unexpectedness of it, caught me off my emotional balance and I felt tears in my throat, blurring my vision, itching on cheeks. She did not seem to notice my odd reaction to her praise.

But, as I said, my memories of Eccles are mainly happy ones. Some of the physical conditions of life in Bardsley Street would probably distress a modern welfare officer, but the year I spent there was the most enjoyable of my childhood. I was well-fed and adequately clothed and, most important, I was secure in the affection of my grandparents. I am still warmed by the memory of my grandmother's tender and indulgent smile. I remember my grandfather's funny songs and the way he always called black puddings 'collier's handcuffs'; I remember his brooding silences, the pungent reek of his pipe and the rare thunder of his rages. I remember Al Jolson at the Regent Cinema, the *Stein Song* and *Bye Bye Blackbird* on Uncle Percy's gramophone; meat and potato pie and dandelion-and-burdock as a treat with Sunday dinner. I remember walking through the churchyard, a short cut to school, treading delicately because the path was paved with flat gravestones. I remember Rismond and Barney Hudson, the Salford football heroes, but only their names, not their presence on the field of play; in summer the little ice-cream cart drawn down the street by a pony, the bell ringing and my running out with a cup to be filled with the delicious stuff which would be eaten with our Sunday tea-time tinned pineapple. I remember longing to have huge hairy forearms and swelling biceps like Uncle Percy's and a great motorbike, like Uncle John's. It was a good year; they were good people to live with, to be protected by, and I did not want to leave them. But my father had rented a photographic studio in Aylesbury, Buckinghamshire, and it was time for the family to reassemble.

*

Aylesbury in the Thirties was a small market town with some light industry on its outskirts. My father's business premises were in the Market Square though, a couple of years after our arrival, we

77

moved to a new and better studio and flat in Kingsbury Square. You might have thought that a luxury trade like photography would have been the last thing to succeed in those penurious days, but Aylesbury and its surrounding countryside has its relatively affluent population and five miles away, near Wendover, was Halton Camp where the RAF trained its apprentices and the young men, peacock-proud in their prickly new uniforms, were eager to spend their money on postcard-sized photographs of themselves. Gradually my father developed a reputation as a good portrait photographer and, for the first time since his marriage at the end of the First World War, the family began to enjoy, if not prosperity, at least relief from the grinding anxieties of extreme poverty.

I went to Queen's Park Boys' Council School which, I suppose, was no better and no worse than most elementary schools of the time. Again I found some difficulty at first in being accepted by groups, though I quickly formed a close and lasting friendship with a tough and adventurous boy called Eddie MacSweeney. After I had taken up boxing at the age of eleven, and especially after I had reached the final of the British Schoolboys' Championships, I was treated by everyone with respect, but it was often an uneasy deference and it did not dispel that persistent sense of being different which had been aggravated on almost my first day at school when my pronunciation of the word 'book' had rocked the classroom with laughter. My year in Eccles had added a dash of the North of England to my mongrel accent and I pronounced the word in the Lancashire way so that the vowel sound was the same as in 'stoop'; evidently the effect of this was richly comic to young Buckinghamshire ears.

Aylesbury was the place where I grew up. I spent nine years there, the years of childhood, puberty and post-adolescence. I do not feel much affection for it although I know that I enjoyed many of the experiences that I first encountered there. Perhaps, in looking back at the place, I identify it with my condition at that time, the uneasiness, self-consciousness, inner conflict and frustration. If the circumstances of my upbringing had been different, if I had been to a better school and perhaps to a university, I might recall the business of growing up with more pleasure, but, as things were, I remember chiefly boredom and frustration which increased as I grew older. At sixteen I looked three or four years more than my age and was able to go into pubs with impunity. I had already developed a taste for beer but I could very rarely afford any since my mother claimed two-thirds of my wages towards the upkeep of the household. Everywhere I saw youths of my own age, nearly all of whom seemed to have far more money to spend than I; they were better dressed and many owned glittering new bicycles and a few even possessed motor-cycles. But more important was my lack of real companionship. After we had left school Eddie and I saw less and less of each other as the grounds of our former intimacy shifted and our interests and aspirations became more widely separated, but there was no one to take his place. I was reading both poetry and prose with pleasure and excitement but there was no friend with whom I could share the thrill of discovery and revelation. And, of course, matters were not improved by sexual anxieties and strangled longings. There were one or two girls, but they were shabby substitutes for the marvellous creatures of my imaginings, and the sweaty and ignorant grapplings beneath the canal bridge on autumnal or wintry nights or in the long grass of summer were, if anything, fuel rather than anodynes for frustration.

When I left school at the age of fourteen I got a job in the offices of a firm of incorporated accountants. Everyone thought I was very lucky because openings of this kind usually went to Grammar School boys and my parents were smugly pleased that my—and by implication their—superiority had been confirmed in this way. I was paid fifteen shillings for a forty-nine hour week three nights of which I attended evening classes in book-keeping, mathematics and something called 'commerce' which, from what I remember, was a very elementary course of economics and business practice. I found these subjects pretty distasteful. I had already decided, on evidence so flimsy that it was perceptible to me alone, that I was going to be a writer, and the only other ambition I seriously entertained was to win a Senior ABA title; the preparation for neither of these activities was of much help to me as an apprentice accountant. My office duties were mechanical and boring: a great deal of filing and copying and compiling of long columns of figures which had to be added up

79

and, in some way which I have long since forgotten, balanced with either the ledgers from which they had been taken or with a bank passbook. I spent quite a lot of the firm's time writing shapeless stories and poem-shaped pieces of nonsense and I often had to take rapid concealing action when the Chief Clerk unexpectedly approached my desk.

There were good things, of course, about Aylesbury: the summer evenings of my schooldays when Eddie and I would swim in the canal and wander home with our towels slung round our necks, making wild and impractical plans for a future of independence and adventure. There were autumn evenings when the darkness came earlier and we would set out on a 'scrumping' expedition, climbing the wall of our chosen victim to help ourselves to apples of a crispness and juiciness such as I have never since tasted. Then the winter, and meetings with Eddie in the small complex of alleys behind the Market Square where we talked of things that thrilled us, of crime, sport, disease, ambitions, girls. In one of the alleys was a small pub, The Dark Lantern, and there was a rumour circulating among us schoolboys that the police had once raided the place and found five couples upstairs doing it. I was not too sure what the 'it' they were doing actually involved, but the mystery added to the excitement and the pub itself had a secretive, conspiratorial look; it was old and timbered, with blind casement windows and an aspect that was vaguely piratical. Two or three years later, when I had left school and looked old enough to be served in pubs, I went into The Dark Lantern, half expecting, with trepidation and excitement, to be invited upstairs by breasty, bold-eyed women to do it with them, but all I found was a small and rather drab bar parlour where the man who sold newspapers in the Market Square was playing dominoes with a cattle-drover, and a couple of RAF sergeants from Halton Camp were playing darts and drinking brown ale.

Perhaps the most vivid of my good memories of Aylesbury is of the Castle Street Hall where the Boxing Club held its training nights. On these evenings I would pack my gear—boxing-boots, vest, trunks, jock-strap and gumshield—and set off through the wintry streets, past St Mary's Church to the old hall and, just before I got there, I would hear the muted sounds from inside, half welcoming and half threatening; then into the brightness and warmth and the strong smell of massage oils. Somebody would be thumping away at the heavy bag and you would hear the rhythmic swish and slap of skipping ropes, the grunts, the slithering feet and the smack of leather on flesh from the boys sparring in the two rings. There was a voluntary, amateur trainer who handled the Juniors in the small ring and Jack Nee who, boxing under the name of Jack Crawford, had been a very good professional featherweight. He was then a corporal at Halton Camp but shortly before the war began he was posted to another station and his job at the Club was taken over by another RAF corporal, Joe Wilby, the reigning ABA Cruiserweight Champion. Wilby was a very nice man, a goodish boxer with a pulverizing left hook, and he was a conscientious trainer, but he could not claim the admiration and devotion I felt for Jack Nee.

Between the ages of fourteen and seventeen I was being painfully torn apart by what seemed the irreconcilable passions for boxing and literature. One part of me wanted to be like Jack, to be tough, jaunty, and fearless and wear badges of scar tissue above my eyes and have a cauliflower ear, while the other part of me wanted to be a young Apollo, like Rupert Brooke, or a Byronic hero, dark, proud and luciferian. The pleasure I took in literature was deep and in no way simulated, yet it was tainted by an irrational feeling that I was indulging in an activity that would have a debilitating effect on me and would prejudice my chances in the ring. It was a silly and unnecessary conflict, but no less troubling for that, and it had its source, I think, in a kind of puritanical suspicion of the arts as something unmanly, emasculating. My father was a good deal to blame here. He was an armchair boxer and he wanted to see his thwarted ambitions or his fantasies realized through his son, and he always had a suspicion of and a distaste for bookishness. Books were all right in their own place and that was the classroom. Out of school a healthy boy should find more manly pleasures to enjoy. One of his frequent admonitions that seemed to reiterate through my early adolescence like a cracked gramophone record was: 'Why don't you go outside and take some exercise? Head always stuck in a book, just like a girl. No wonder you've got spots!'

By the time I was eighteen I was no longer troubled by these objurgations and I had come to see that it was foolish to be self-conscious about the apparent contradiction of interests in boxing and literature, that in fact I was lucky to be able to get pleasure from them both. But I did not win my Senior ABA Title, or even enter for the championships, because the war against Hitler had begun and I was shortly to start training for a different kind of fighting.

NOW

I T IS a fine day, bright sunshine and fluffy dumplings of very white cloud in a dark blue sky. This evening I have to go to Dorchester to lay a wreath on Thomas Hardy's monument and then give a talk to the Hardy Society. I am flattered to be asked but I see little point in societies of this kind, unless they are promoting serious research and perhaps discovering unpublished material. Mostly they seem to be made up of mildly fanatical people who have chosen Hardy, Browning, the Brontës or whoever their champion may be, not through any great desire to know more about an author for whom they feel a special veneration, not even because they greatly love his work or have even read it with any thoroughness (a prominent member of the Hardy Society told me he does not read poetry, not Hardy's nor anyone else's) but from a devotion to a particular region or perhaps to a philosophical, religious or political conviction which they, often wrongly, consider central to the writer's work. But regional chauvinism is, I think, the common motive for joining these organizations. There must be thousands of Scotsmen who attend Burns suppers yet would not know more than a few lines of the poetry, and the verses they might be familiar with would almost certainly be the worst of their hero, the sententious, moralizing stuff and not the vigorous Villonesque or the fine lyrical poetry.

Still, I am quite glad to be asked to give the talk—which is to be about Hardy's poetry—because, in the preparation of it, I have re-read a lot of Hardy's work which I have for too long neglected, and with no less pleasure than before. At his best he is quite magnificent and there is no poet quite like him. The much too common academic view that he is a man who wrote a handful of authentic poems among a huge mass of inferior or even positively bad verse seems to me stupidly wide of the mark. What is astonishing is that so much of his

83

vast output should be so splendid and that so little of it is negligible.

The occasion of the wreath-laying is the anniversary of his birth, June 2. In four days' time it will be the twenty-sixth anniversary of D-Day, the allied invasion of Normandy. Over a quarter of a century! Can it possibly be so long ago? I was about to say '. . . so long ago, yet I remember it in such clear detail when events which happened only the other week have completely faded from memory.' But on reflection, I realize that I do not remember it so clearly after all. History remembers it, and I remember it as history, but of my own part only certain fragments are fixed in the memory, fragments, too, which, on the surface, are not particularly spectacular or significant. And it is the same with the whole of the war: I could not be trusted to give a reliable account of the events of any military action that I took part in because I have no recollection of the occasion as a whole. What I retain is a few images, often irrelevant to the main issue, and, if I am to be honest, in writing about my own experience of war I can only present it in a fragmentary way.

I do not know whether other people who took an active part in battles find the same thing—from some personal accounts of the war that I have read it would seem otherwise—but, when I try to recall various attacks and smaller skirmishes, it seems that I went through them in a kind of trance and I have since wondered if I was not indeed in some kind of self-induced hypnotic state which preserved me from panic and disintegration. On the other hand it might be that my memory is refusing to recall much of what happened because it knows that such recollection would not be good for me. Of something like eighteen months of action in the Western Desert, Tripolitania and Tunisia I remember, in precise detail, not more than a few hours, though the experience has left in the memory a shifting impressionistic canvas of enormous size but seen in bad light and from too far away. Similarly, I was in Normandy for only three weeks but I can remember incidents that would account for only the minutest fraction of that time, and it is surprising how few of these images are spectacularly violent, dramatic or frightening. It is almost as if the inner recording eye had fixed itself on phenomena that the mind would be able to live with in the future without too much distress.

THEN

Laying Mines

I am not sure where we were. It might have been at Zem-Zem or it might have been later, when we had passed Tripoli and were facing the Germans in the Mareth Line. I shared a slit-trench with MacCabe, a thickset Glaswegian who, when we were being shelled and were sitting, knees up to our chins and face to face in the trench, would stick the end of his index finger into his mouth and blow, with distended cheeks and bulging eyes, as if he were giving a prolonged blast on a whistle; and, as he blew, his steel helmet would seem to rise and stay suspended an inch or two above his head. It was an effective trick performed by exerting pressure on the rear brim of his helmet against the wall of the trench behind him, forcing the front of the helmet upwards, and it was his answer to the problem of how to behave when mortally terrified. It was a problem that we all had to solve in our different ways. Some of us adopted a pose of tough insouciance, some abandoned all attempts at dissimulation and gritted their teeth and closed their eyes and muttered broken prayers, half-remembered from childhood, while others grew blasphemous, swollen with rage and the impotent lust to smash— not the Germans—but the real enemy, the obscene and humiliating terror that mauled every one of us. MacCabe's defence was buffoonery and he was a good man to share a trench with.

It was night. The ration truck had been up and we had sneaked out, one at a time, over the sand with our mess-tins and mugs to return with tinned potatoes and stew, rice and mugs of milkless tea. We ate, and I drank half of my tea and poured the other half into my water-bottle to drink in the early hours of the morning when I would be parched and the tea would be cold and delicious as nectar. Things were fairly quiet: in the distance the stammered dialogue of Bren and

85

Spandau as patrols made contact, the flash and rumble of distant artillery. Then our platoon-sergeant crawled over to us and crouched on the parapet of the trench and said, 'Right. You men's on mine-laying. Follow me jildy. We got to get going while things is quiet.'

We followed him to his trench where the rest of the section was gathered and he handed out a dozen anti-personnel mines to each of us. I forget what the mines were called: Mark something-or-other. They were flask-shaped, flat with a raised portion on the surface into which the detonators were inserted and which needed only a few pounds pressure to set them off. We moved out in front of our positions and the sergeant told us where to lay the mines. You scraped a declivity in the sand and placed your mine in it and covered it over quite lightly. We worked as quickly and quietly as we could. The enemy was not far away though how close their forward positions were we did not know.

I had finished laying my mines when the sergeant whispered: 'We need another dozen. Nip back and get them, will you.'

I returned to his trench and found the mines. I was carrying them back to the others, holding them, one on top of the other against my chest like a pile of books, my chin lightly steadying the uppermost one, when the careful silence was suddenly cut through by the whining noise of mortars hurling through the air. Two of the bombs exploded twenty or so yards away. There was another, shriller swooping noise and this time I knew the bomb was for me, its menace was focused and personal. I was its single target. The blast slammed at my ears, earth sprayed and, involuntarily, I ducked and defensive hands came up to protect my head and eyes. My load of high explosive was scattered on the ground as I went down for cover. The bang in my skull faded and I could smell very close the sweet and deadly reek of cordite. Miraculously I had escaped being hit by shrapnel from the mortar-bomb and, even more miraculously, not one of my mines had blown up.

The sergeant came over as I was collecting the mines together ''kin 'ell,' he hissed. 'What you think you're on? Trying to blow the whole fucking lot of us to bits?'

We finished laying the mines and the mortar fire continued as we scurried back to the dubious safety of our slit trenches.

MacCabe crouched low in the trench, his head down and his hands carefully sheltering the glow of the cigarette-end he had just lit. You had to be very careful over smoking because the burning tip of a cigarette could be seen at night from an extraordinary distance.

He said, 'Christ, you're a lucky bastard, dropping that lot. I thought you was going to make bully beef hash out the lot of us. Aye, you're a lucky bastard, all right, and one thing's for sure. I'm going to stick close to you from now on. I'm telling you. If you can get away with that, you can get away with anything. I'm going to be your shadow when the shit's flying.'

But he did not stick close enough and a few weeks later he tripped an S-mine and both of his legs were blown off. I never found out whether he survived the war or not.

Mock Attack

It was early in 1943, around February or perhaps early March, and we had been pulled out of the line for baths in the mobile showers and to get rid of our lice-infested clothing and be issued with fresh deloused battle-dress, for at night it was cold and we were not wearing khaki drill. As darkness fell we watched the lunar phases with concern because we knew that General Montgomery favoured a full moon for an attack and we sensed that an attack was imminent. During the day we lazed around and at tiffin we experimented with our ration of hard tack, crushing it down and mixing it with water and jam to make a kind of pudding. We smoked our V cigarettes and played cards and talked about home and girls and what a lot we earned in civvy street. A few stray shells from the German eighty-eights sighed overhead and crunched the earth up somewhere on our flank. We were safe, briefly and precariously, but memories of previous, and fears of future engagements were never quite out of sight.

On the day of the move, we knew something was going to happen. O Groups were held, there was a lot of running about between Company and Battalion H.Q.s and despatch-riders would take off for or arrive from the rear echelons of Brigade and Divisional Head-quarters. Then, in the late afternoon, we other ranks were paraded and told by the Company Commander that we were going to make a mock attack that night. A mock attack: it sounded quite comforting; not a real attack but an exercise like one of those schemes we used to do back in Blighty, using blank ammunition and getting back to barracks or camp for sausage and chips in the NAAFI. But the mock attack was not like that at all. It was a kind of feint where the Brigade moved forward behind an artillery barrage just as if we were putting in a proper attack, but instead of trying to get to grips with the enemy we would dig in before we reached their forward positions. The aim was to distract the Germans while the New Zealanders made a flanking movement to get round to the back of the Mareth Line and cut off the line of retreat.

As we were dismissed, the Company Sergeant-major told me to stay behind.

He said, 'Got a nice wee job for you tonight. Bruce, the Company Runner, he's gone sick, got a touch of sandfly. You'll be taking his place tonight. You join the Company Commander at the starting line and stick with him like his third arm.'

We spent the rest of the hours of daylight in cleaning and checking weapons and, as darkness was falling, we were given a hot meal for which I had little appetite. Against the dark skyline the enemy guns flickered and rumbled like an approaching storm. Excitement and apprehension were in the air like the electric charge that presages a violent cataclysm. We made sure we had our field-dressings and we assembled our equipment, the small pack, ammunition pouches, belt and bayonet. Then we climbed aboard the trucks that were to take us up to the starting-line. The convoy moved off, lurching and labouring in the dust, rubble and sand. Nobody said much. There were one or two lugubrious jokes but no laughter

One of the things that never lost its power to surprise was the sheer absurdity of a large-scale military operation, the white tape at the starting point, parodying a school sports day, the way we crouched there at the tape as our barrage began its skull-bulging din from behind and then the Germans replying, the sound of our first casualty, somewhere over on my left, his voice shrill and naked, yelling over and over again: 'Oh, Jesus Christ! Oh, mother! Oh, mother! Help me, Christ! Oh, Jesus! Oh, mother, mother . . .' going on and on, and one wishing above all things that he would

88

shut up, even if silence meant his drowning in the blackness of his death.

While we still lay trembling and wincing and praying, the Scorpions, big tanks with flails for digging up mines, went through the enemy minefield and then engineers put down parallel white tapes to mark the path of comparative safety that the attacking infantry must use. I saw the Company Commander look at his watch and a few seconds later he stood up and blew a whistle and I rose, too, and followed him as the Company started to advance towards the opening in the minefield. We had moved forward for about thirty or forty yards when things started to go wrong. Our artillery was putting down a creeping barrage behind which we were meant to advance but somebody had made a mistake in timing; either we had begun to advance too soon or the gunners were not increasing their range quickly enough and we found ourselves halfway through the minefield being plastered by our twenty-five pounders from behind and by the German eighty-eights from ahead. A demand for a smoke-screen must have been sent back because smoke-shells came over and when the acrid stuff began to claw at our eyes and throats someone shouted, 'Gas! They're using gas!' and there was a moment of panic before the C.S.M. was heard roaring, 'It's smoke, you bloody fool! It's smoke!'

A Spandau machine gun had got a fixed line on the gap at the other end of the minefield and was firing regular bursts. You could see the tracers like red-hot embers sliding through the dark. Shells were exploding all around us and you could hear cries and moans from the wounded and the stink of cordite was both harsh and sweet in the nostrils and throat. The Company Commander and I went to ground and took cover, lying side by side, flat on our faces. There seemed even more of the heavy stuff coming over and all around us the earth was heaving and grunting and throwing up plumes of sand and stones and you could hear the white-hot shrapnel chirring through the air above your head. The machine-gun battalion of the Middlesex Regiment started yammering away on their Vickers guns. My face was pressed to the earth, eyes and teeth clamped tight. I do not know how long it was before I sneaked a look at the Company Commander, hoping to God that he did not need me to run any messages to other Companies. He did not. He did not need me for anything. He was not there. He had taken a powder, got off his mark, vamoosed, or in the more formal language of military jurisprudence, he had deserted in the face of the enemy.

I thought seriously about taking a powder myself but I guessed that I would receive a less sympathetic hearing than the Company Commander if ever I reached the relative safety of a rear echelon without being shot by one side or the other. There was only one thing to do. I got hold of my entrenching tool and began to dig myself a trench, there where I was on the minefield path, and I sweated and panted and laboured until it was deep enough to afford me reasonable shelter from bullets and shrapnel, and I crawled into it to wait until somebody in authority arrived to tell me what to do or until one of those shells scored a direct hit and solved all my problems, then and for ever.

I never saw the Company Commander again. A long time afterwards I heard from a lance-corporal who had been wounded in the mock attack that he had seen the gallant captain in Tripoli where he had been hospitalized as bomb-happy and subsequently given an administrative job and promoted to major.

Adolf

Before we embarked for the invasion of Normandy the Battalion was under canvas at a place called Grays, near Tilbury. We were surrounded by barbed wire and there were guards of Military Police outside the wire, not to stop anyone getting in but to prevent us from getting out and running for cover. In memory, the weather was continuously fine, and we played football and lay around in the sun, bored yet tense, liable to fits of absurd gaiety or outbursts of irrational bad temper. Discipline was not easy to enforce because what, under other circumstances, might have been a potent threat of detention was now regarded by many of us a desirable reprieve from very probable execution on the beaches of Normandy. Some of the young recruits who had joined the Battalion on its return from the Middle East were excited by the prospect of action but we old hands, with our Africa Stars and wound stripes, listened to their prattle with sour amusement. They would learn.

On the day before embarkation we were paid in the afternoon and it was understood that we would enjoy a booze-up in the evening, our last gutful of English beer for a long time, perhaps our last ever. As soon as the NAAFI tent was opened it was packed with soldiers armed with tea pails and fire buckets, all showing a fierce and single-minded determination to get their vessels filled with beer that their less experienced officers might hopefully, and misguidedly, have interpreted as an encouraging sign for the forthcoming adventure. The uneasiness that you could feel in the camp's atmosphere over the past week or so had now sharpened: a sense of leashed hysteria moved in the air, an electric feeling like the shadow of a crouching storm, a nervous and dangerous hilarity, a half-drawn glint of anarchy and rebellion. The drinking was done methodically and fast and we put away many gallons of beer.

When the NAAFI packed up, or dried up, we went back to our tents, if we still had beer left in our buckets; or if we had finished all our drink we roamed the lines looking for hospitality or entertainment. There was a lot of singing, sentimental or bawdy, and every now and then you would hear one of those mad shrieking whoops that drunken soldiers release, a wild noise that has in it something of defiance, exultation and despair. In the tent my companions were singing, jabbering nonsense or vomiting. The Orderly Sergeant came round and ordered us to get our heads down, but he was told to fuck off. Then somebody said, 'Let's get Adolf. Let's give Adolf a bouncing!' Adolf was the nickname of our platoon commander, a stout young man with a black moustache that made his teeth look very white when he put on his snarling grin which looked to us both supercilious and cruel but was probably evidence of nervousness. He was not liked by the men in his platoon. The soldier who had suggested giving him a bouncing had grabbed a blanket. 'Come on!' he yelled. 'Get fell in the lynching party!' A dozen or so noisy soldiers advanced unsteadily on the officer's tent.

Adolf had probably enjoyed a convivial evening in the Mess and he was tucked up in his camp bed when the lynching party arrived. At first he tried to jolly his way out of what was in store for him . . . 'All right, chaps. You've had your fun. Don't blame you a bit. Had a few noggins myself but it's time for bye-byes now. Tomorrow's going to be a—No! I mean it. Damn it, you'll—let go of me! Let go! That's an order! Damn you, I'll see you all in—I know who you are —You'll all be on—Help! Put me down! You swine, put me down!'

He was not put down but carried, struggling wildly and mouthing oaths and threats, and dumped on to the spread blanket whose edges were grasped by eight or nine pairs of hands. At a concerted cry of 'Ups-he-goes!' he was tossed high in the air to fall back into the blanket. Up he went again, even higher, shouting hoarse and incomprehensible protests and appeals as he descended, clutching at the air like a giant frog or free-fall parachutist. Again he was tossed, again and again, higher and higher, the blanket-wielders sweating and roaring and staggering. Then, either by design or accident, one end of the blanket gave way as he came down from a height of twelve feet or so. His fall could have been broken scarcely at all and he thumped shudderingly on to the ground, landing with a great shout of shock and pain and then lying there moaning as the party broke up and fled back to their tents. No one stayed to see what sort of shape poor Adolf was in.

Soon after dawn next day the battalion paraded in battle-order, ready to move off in trucks to Tilbury where the landing craft were waiting for us to go aboard. Adolf was there, looking pale and viciously dignified, moving with an awkward limp. We were inspected by the C.O. and then we climbed into the trucks. I had a bad hangover, as I expect most of us had, and perhaps it was this that helped to deaden fear. The machinery had been set in motion and there was nothing to be done about it. Cigarettes were lit but nobody said much. There was something unreal, something dream-like about events; when we got to the docks we seemed to move slowly and wordlessly like somnambulists. The feeling of sick apprehension that had intermittently troubled us during the previous few weeks had given way to a feeling that was a mixture of resignation and disbelief. My intelligence had understood that I would soon be killed or maimed but the message was censored before it reached the imagination so that it was almost without meaning. We had been issued with strong paper bags to be sick into on voyage. I was Number One on the Bren. We were going to France. And nothing seemed real. I wondered how the bruised and limping Adolf felt. I would not have been surprised to learn that he hated the men in his platoon far more than he hated the Germans.

He was wounded in the throat by shrapnel on D-Day plus two and was taken back to the Casualty Clearing Station at Arromanches and from there back to safety and clean sheets in Blighty. Lucky Adolf. I wonder if his most vivid memory of June 1944 is an incident, not from the landing or the fighting, but one which occurred on the night before embarkation when he was tossed like a giant pancake under the stars by the men whom he was to command in battle.

Landscape with Figures

Normandy was green, sylvan and fruitful; it was cider country, rather like Dorset. But the fields were strewn with dead cattle, killed by shrapnel or by blast from the shells that had pitted the beautiful meadows. Some of the carcasses of the beasts were swollen almost to bursting point and the legs stuck out, ludicrous and stiff as broomsticks. The smell of putrefaction, sweet and pungent, a little like burning candle grease but sharper, sickened the summer air. The trees were luxuriant but their foliage often concealed snipers. The German snipers were accurate shots and they were dedicated men. They would keep on firing, picking off their targets, until they were spotted; and then their hiding places would be sprayed by bursts from Sten or Bren and they would tumble out of the branches. Our own snipers favoured discretion and were more interested in survival than in reducing German military strength.

The platoon occupied a deserted farm for a few hours and in the cellar of the house we found barrels of cider and a few bottles of Calvados. Our sergeant sensibly rationed the drink, but he was not stingy and he made sure that each man received enough to keep fear and despondency at a tolerable distance. With great caution, because of the danger of booby-traps, we explored the house and found in an upper room, lying in bed, a woman. She was an old woman and she was dead. There were no marks on her that we could see, so we assumed that she had died from natural causes, perhaps from heart failure when the noise of the invasion began, and that her body had been left behind as a burdensome irrelevance when the farmer and his household set out on the exodus towards the coast.

*

After dark you could see the tracers of the anti-aircraft guns firing back near the beach. The Bofors seemed to be juggling with fiery oranges, tossing them rapidly up, high into the sky, never dropping one. In more peaceful moments I would indulge in fantasies of returning to the coast and somehow smuggling myself back to England. I wondered what crazy aberration of the mind had made me forget those times of terror in the desert, why I was here at all, why, for that matter, any of us who had already known warfare were so insane as to return. Fear is perhaps the most humiliating experience man can undergo and that is why he so quickly forgets its anguish. There can be nothing more emasculating, nothing more obscene and murderous than the pure physical terror that savages you when loud and violent death is screaming down from the sky and pounding the earth around you, smashing and pulping everything in its search for you.

In Normandy I dug in with a man called Bill Grey who was the fastest man with a spade I have ever known. Even on hard ground he could dig, in a very few minutes, a trench deep enough for us both to protect our heads when the shit was flying. The Germans used a seven-barrelled mortar that we called Moaning Minnie because of the siren-like wailing it made when it released, almost simultaneously, its seven bombs. We suffered a lot from these weapons and I was often grateful to Bill for his trench-digging ability.

He came from Banffshire and he wished that he had never left. He was a romantic who had been slammed face to face with a particularly appalling reality and he was on the edge of going to pieces. So far, his sense of humour had preserved him but I wondered how long it would keep him going. He could still occasionally laugh at his own terror, but his laughter was becoming rarer and fainter and his fear stronger and almost unceasing in its depredations.

He had joined the Battalion in the Mareth Line, straight from a cushy pen-pushing job in Palestine which he had found boring and

94

shameful and from which he had repeatedly asked to be released and transferred to a fighting unit. At last his wish had been granted and he was sent with a batch of reinforcements to the Gordons. It took him, he told me after we had become friends, about ten minutes in a forward area to realize that he had made a colossal blunder, and the fact that he had only his own folly to blame did not alleviate his distress.

He was not, in the ordinary way, a physical coward; he was a very good soccer player and, though not temperamentally aggressive, he was unafraid of bodily violence and I had once seen him handle a drunken and pugnacious sailor with decisive efficiency. There is, of course, no reliable way of judging the intensity of another man's fear. Perhaps every soldier in his first experience of battle feels the same initial drench of terror, but each one varies greatly in his capacity for modifying it, for making it tolerable, according to his training, environment, temperament, perhaps hereditary characteristics and even, possibly, his chemistry.

The theory that I have often heard expounded that the man with scant imaginative power is the man most likely to react to battle conditions with the greatest equanimity does not seem to me acceptable, for the soldier who possesses an active imagination can rehearse in his mind the ordeal that lies ahead of him, and it could even transpire that the reality of the experience might be so much less horrific than the scenes he has enacted in imagination that he would acquit himself with reasonable assurance, if not distinction. The unimaginative man, the man without resources to prepare himself for the test, might be shocked into panic at the first and totally unexpected assault on nerves and senses. I am not sure. It is probably foolish to generalize, though we did have, in our platoon, one man who seemed to support this tentative belief of mine.

Robbie was a large, clumsy boy from Aberdeen with a big featureless face like a lumpy peeled potato crowned with coarse dull hair. He was the squad butt, natural target for the drill-sergeant's formalized, half-jocular invective. I do not think he could read or write and he did not even find brief escape from his wretched existence through the anodynes of alcohol, tobacco or sex. The other men would occasionally tease him, but not cruelly, and there was usually someone to help him when he could not manage the fastenings of his equipment or when he was uncertain where he should go or what he should do. He was one of the reinforcements who had joined us on our return from the Middle East, all of them about eighteen years of age and with only twelve weeks' or so service at a training depot. Normandy was, of course, his first experience of action.

We were in a field, in or near Ranville, and one night the Company was pinned down by heavy mortar fire. We crouched in our trenches in the darkness as the Moaning Minnies howled and whined over and burst all around us. For most of the night the barrage continued but the expected infantry attack from the Germans did not take place. As the night thinned and dawn stirred and began to breathe its cold grey breath into the failing darkness, the mortars tired from their labours and there was an uneasy silence. Helmeted heads peered over the parapets of trenches in our field. Slowly we emerged from our holes and began to check the area for casualties. It seemed incredible that there were so few after the lambasting we had endured. Five wounded, and only one of them badly, and two killed. One of the dead was Robbie, but he had not been killed by mortar fire. He had managed to get the muzzle of his own rifle into his mouth and had blown away most of his head.

*

The name of the place was, I think, Toufreville, or perhaps that was the site of some other incident. It does not matter. It was a small town and, like most places in Normandy, it had been badly smashed up by artillery and aerial bombardment. The Battalion had dug in overnight in a wood on the town's outskirts. We did not know whether or not it was occupied by the enemy so, after daybreak, a reconnaissance patrol was sent forward with a platoon sergeant in charge.

The air was bright and fragrant with sunshine and freshness. The only thing that prevented this early summer morning from being typical was the silence: the birds and their songs had departed to more peaceful places and most of the farm livestock had been killed. In many of the fields great stakes had been driven into the ground

96

in close-set patterns to frustrate the landing of troop-carrying gliders, and we had seen many broken-backed craft with crushed wings lying like enormous crippled birds in the gentle pastureland.

We kept close to the hedges and moved with caution. The silence was unnerving. It was not merely the absence of sound; it was a presence, a positive threat; it seemed to make breathing more difficult as if its weight had displaced the oxygen in the air. A sudden noise would have been intolerable to our tensed nerves. But there was no noise as we entered the town and made our dodging, scurrying progress from doorway to doorway of shattered and deserted houses until we had reached the centre, the Place. There was no living person there, but there were plenty of dead.

In the middle of the Place was a small public garden with trees and from many of these hung dead British paratroopers, suspended from branches by their harnesses, who had evidently been picked off by small arms fire as they hung helplessly there. On the lawns and flower beds of the garden, too, were more dead soldiers wearing the flashes of the Sixth Airborne Division, and others lay on the cobbled stones outside the little park. None was alive. They lay with that stillness which is more still than the motionlessness of inanimate objects, station, rank and quality now irrelevant, anonymous and democratized, even their pathos reduced by uniformity.

We went into one of the deserted cafés and helped ourselves to bottles of Calvados before we headed out of the town, back to our positions. We felt no shame at leaving those airborne soldiers behind, only a nervous gratitude for our own survival. It was only later that guilt began, that those hanging paratroopers and their sprawled comrades on the ground began their ceaseless whispers of accusation.

*

It was night and we crouched in our slit trenches on either side of a rough road near the Caen Canal. We were in support of an attack that was being put in by one of the other brigades in the division. If they took their positions we would move forward in daylight and consolidate them, be fresh to repel a possible counter-attack. We were not feeling fresh. I was so tired that I had literally fallen asleep on the march.

Bill Grey and I were on the Bren. I was Number One and his job was to keep the magazines clean and loaded and feed them to me when I was firing.

He said, 'You get some kip. I'll keep guard. If I want to sleep I'll give you a shake later on.'

The barrage started up and the machine-guns jabbered at each other in the darkness that was gashed with flashes from the artillery and intermittently hung with flares. I was so tired that the din was almost soporific and I slept, crouching in the trench in the foetal position, while Bill leaned on the parapet with the Bren gun and peered out anxiously for sign of hostile movement. The Germans had a disturbing way of filtering through our forward positions and doing a lot of damage from behind.

It was almost daybreak when Bill woke me up.

'I'm out on my feet,' he said. 'I've got to get some sleep.'

I rubbed the muck from my eyes, took a swig from the water-bottle and rinsed out my mouth. My face felt stiff as if I had been wearing a dried mud-pack. I lit a cigarette and told Bill to get his head down. Within seconds he was snoring quietly. The trees seemed to rise spectrally from the ground as the darkness gave way to mist which hung in wisps from branch and hedgerow. The air was cold and clean, sharp in the nostrils. Presently I could make out the shattered signpost a hundred yards or so away where a German dispatch-rider lay still clutching the handlebars of his bike. The sigh and thump of shellfire were irregular, almost desultory, as if the battle, like a tired machine, had almost run down and was sputtering to a final stillness. Then I heard the noise of motor engines and a few moments later there appeared beyond the signpost, where there was a bend in the road, a couple of jeeps carrying stretchers fixed above the heads of the drivers, and flying Red Cross pennants. They were followed almost at once by a small convoy of ambulances which passed slowly, heading for the Casualty Clearing Station back at Arromanches. After they had gone there was nothing to be seen on the road for ten minutes or more and then the first batch of walking wounded appeared.

There was something haunting about the sight of those men, all wounded yet not badly enough to be on stretchers, making their way back to have their injuries treated and then almost certainly to be returned to the forward area to face again further ordeals of the kind they had just survived. Seen through the veils of mist, there was something moving, something archetypal about the frieze-like procession. They moved like sleep-walkers; they were shocked and exhausted and their eyes had about them a remote, stunned look, as if they were still gazing upon the scenes of carnage that had raged about them on the previous night. For those few moments as they walked slowly past, they seemed to possess a symbolic power: they were the representatives, not only of the military victims of war but of suffering and innocent people everywhere and at all times, trapped in the skeins of historical necessity. I was affected by the sight of those men in a way that I had not been affected by more dramatic and spectacular events, and the memory of the walking wounded on that road near the Caen Canal has been fixed in my memory ever since.

After they had gone we got the order to move forward and, soon afterwards, I was wounded and taken back to England.

NOW

REAL summer weather now, warm and indolent, seducing one away from the little winter of industrious self-application. I put Delius on the record-player and sun myself in the garden like a Rajah. I try not to hate myself because I am suffering from a hangover but I cannot help but feel soiled and frayed, unworthy of the gift of such an afternoon as this.

It must be difficult for rational, non-drinking people to understand why heavy drinkers go on knocking themselves out with alcohol, wasting countless hours in bars, squandering money, energy and even, sometimes, wit and invention, and then, the next day or in the case of large-scale booze-ups over the next two or three days, suffering fairly intense physical and mental distress. I have sometimes wondered if the hangover is not unconsciously desired by the boozer, that he feels a need for it just as some people gamble heavily because they crave the punishment of losing, for both the hangover—about which I know quite a lot—and the compulsive gambler's reckless plunges into the sense of loss—about which I can only guess—seem to me experiences that offer parallels with, or perhaps parodies of, mystical states of consciousness; and most of us, who are deprived through lack of faith of the more orthodox and authentic forms of religious experience, are still assailed, perhaps more often than we know, by 'a hunger . . . to be more serious'.

Some drugs, they say, can induce visions, the sense of the numinous, something approaching the saint's or the shaman's sense of identity with his deity or deities, but alcohol does not do anything like this, at least not for me. It releases and relaxes and sometimes lends a precarious and doomed state of euphoria. It is the hangover that seems to induce a state that is related, however obliquely and distantly, to mystical experience, not the mystical ecstatic but its dark reverse, a condition not so very different in kind, I imagine, from what Saint John of the Cross meant by the 'dark night of the soul'. I am sure that this will sound grotesquely exaggerated to the teetotaller and sacrilegious to the devout, but I have known hang-overs when I have been filled with a sense of self-disgust, feelings of unfocused anxiety and terrible loneliness which cannot be so very different from the anguished Christian's feeling of separation from God. I have also experienced a kind of waking nightmare that does not vary: it occurs when I am on the edges of sleep but still awake. It has no narrative, no local setting. As soon as my eyes are closed a face moves towards me, comes near, recedes and is followed by another, a procession of faces of indescribable evil. They are like living gargoyles but infinitely more bestial and they bring with them an effluence of terror and vileness, something that is part taste and part stench but not properly either, a sulphurous reek in the head.

There may be probably a plausible psychological or physio-logical explanation for these manifestations, but when the things occur they are terrifying and sickening and they make one under-stand very well what Gerard Manley Hopkins meant in the poem beginning: 'I wake and feel the fell of dark . . .' when he cries: 'I am gall, I am heartburn. God's most deep decree/ Bitter would have me taste: my taste was me.' All this may seem fanciful, pre-tentious if not completely barmy, but at least it offers the glimmer of an answer to the question of why one persists in regular bouts of drinking, knowing that they will be followed by the misery of hang-overs that murder the capacity for work, constructive thought and even the enjoyment of the simplest things.

Today's hangover is not really a bad one, lassitude and vague depression are the worst symptoms, but I feel cheated because I did not much enjoy my drinking last night which was prompted by despair at the political stupidity of the very nice men in the local who had, to a man and entirely against their own interests as underpaid manual workers, voted for the Conservatives in the recent election. I might have drunk too much anyway, but there is no doubt that the Tory victory has made me feel miserable and misanthropic. Not that I am a political animal at all. My support of the Labour

Party is, I suppose, sentimentally motivated. I know that I am lazy, mean, covetous and acquisitive. I know that if I were wealthy I would be as keen as anyone to retain and, if possible, increase my wealth. It is not likely that I would be prepared voluntarily to make do with less so that the circumstances of others less fortunate than myself would be improved. I might, as a sop to conscience, write an occasional cheque to one of the well-advertised charities, but I am pretty sure I would not make over a regular and substantial part of my income so that social inequality might be a little redressed and suffering a little alleviated. And I do not believe, alas, that I am unusual in my selfishness and greed.

Since many, indeed most, people are like this I feel that they should be forced by law to contribute a fair proportion of their wealth to help the less lucky or gifted, the less strong or cunning, towards a comparable standard of living. If we are not generous, fair, tolerant and sympathetic by nature, then we should be compelled to behave as if we were. I know that this is a naïve attitude to politics and that it might seem to advocate too great a degree of State interference with the rights of the individual to make his own moral choices, to accept feebly the obliteration of individuality and to welcome the apotheosis of mediocrity. Then I shall be asked what paragons are going to be entrusted with the legislation of enforced virtue and I can only answer that history has shown that there have always been a fair number of public-spirited people in each generation, people who possess a rawness of social conscience, a gnawing indignation at the spectacle of exploitation and injustice, and that they have been prepared more or less selflessly to dedicate their lives to the amelioration of such wrongs. And as for the 'levelling down' that socialism is so often accused of promoting, the puritanical reduction of the unorthodox and individual to a uniform drabness, I think it is enough to note that these charges almost invariably come from men and women of blood-freezing conformity and unoriginality.

Quite simply, I am angered at living in a society that allows its less favoured members to exist at a material level many many fathoms below a reasonable norm and I gibber with rage when I hear vinous, steak-fed gentlemen, usually engaged in wholly unproductive and non-creative professions, inveighing against the laziness and greed of dustmen, transport workers, miners and the like who are so insolent as to demand a minimum weekly wage that is probably less than one tenth of the income enjoyed by the stockbrokers, lawyers and middlemen of one kind or another who bleat and bumble about the idleness of the workers and the irresponsibility of the Unions.

The alleviation of extreme poverty is not, of course, a guarantee of a happy life but it at least makes contentment a possibility. I suppose that, by the standards of many people, I am a poor man, but I count myself very lucky that I live in a house large enough to contain without too much discomfort my wife and five children who have never known serious material deprivation; but I also count myself lucky that I have known in the past real poverty, for if I had not I would be far less grateful and contented with my present circumstances than I am.

THEN

WHEN I was discharged from Northfield Military Hospital in late 1947 I went back to Leeds and found, near the University, a comfortable room in a large house which was occupied mainly by students who paid low rents and practised mutual aid over such matters as financial loans, the sharing of food, drink and even clothes. I wore my demob suit, a grey chalk-stripe of uncertain fit and I had about sixty pounds of my gratuity left, so I felt no pressing need to look for a job. My closest Leeds friend, Kenneth Severs, had left for Durham where he was teaching at Hatfield College, but there were plenty of old relationships to be renewed and new ones to be cemented.

I drank in The Pack Horse, Whitelocks or The Jubilee with R. C. Scriven, who was known by everyone as Ratz, and we were often joined by Wilfred Childe who was a member of the English Faculty at Leeds and who wrote poetry of great decorative elaboration, a kind of stained-glass mysticism and a verbal softness and sweetness like melting marzipan. The poetry was awful, but the man was very good indeed: his taste was surprisingly wide-ranging in view of the limitations and deficiencies of his own work. He had a nice, quiet sense of humour. One evening we were drinking in Whitelocks when John Braine, who was then living near Bradford and had yet to make his name as a popular novelist, began to blast the dullness and conventionality of the Bradford middle classes. He wound up his diatribe by exclaiming: 'They think exactly alike—if you can call it thinking. They talk alike. They even look exactly alike.'

'That must be rather confusing,' Wilfred murmured, unnoticed by Braine.

Wilfred lived in a large musty Victorian house in Harrogate and he had filled almost every room with books, not always regimented in shelves but in some cases piled quite literally to the roof. He was a generous man and he lent or gave me many works which would otherwise have been difficult or impossible to obtain. His scholarly and religious preoccupations and his own curiously overwrought verse did not prevent him from taking an interest in contemporary literature, especially contemporary poetry, and I have never quite been able to understand how a man who could relish the work of Auden and Empson, Dylan Thomas and George Barker could persist in producing such quantities of fustian. He was quick, as well, to spot the promise of young and, at the time, almost unknown writers, and he gave extra-mural encouragement and free beer to those of his students who wrote what he thought was original work with potential. We were quite often joined on our pub evenings by a protégé of his, an intense and enthusiastic young man named Robin Skelton.

Just before my money completely ran out I got a job in the editorial department of E. J. Arnold and Son, the educational publishers who operate from Leeds, and there I spent eight hours a day reading proofs, doing some rewriting and abridging the 'classics', so it was not surprising that, after the day's work, I felt disinclined to go back to my room and read or write. I stuck the job for a few months then, partly through boredom with the routine and partly because I was spending all my spare time and money in pubs and getting no work of my own done, I left and joined the staff of a small preparatory school on the outskirts of Leeds.

Teaching allowed me more time and inclination for my writing and I sold a few poems to magazines and, in 1948, brought out a woolly and wordy collection of poems, one or two of which, to my grave embarrassment, still turn up occasionally in anthologies. A love affair which had been going on sporadically since my days on the run was coming to an untidy and abrasive conclusion and a fresh one, which promised more distress than delight for both of us, was in those early stages when retreat, though painful, is still a possibility. Leeds was changing, or my relationship with Leeds was changing. I still found beauty in its ugliness, I still felt gratitude for its warmth, but it seemed smaller now and too constricting. There were times when I felt that I had to get away from its voice, its manners, its features. Some of my friends seemed too readily satisfied with what Leeds could offer them, assuming too easily that no other place could offer them more. Some, without knowing it, had been defeated by Leeds, been reduced and exhausted by it, afflicted by that most insidious of provincial diseases, a complacent impotence. I felt disloyal and a little guilty, but I had to go. And of course there seemed only one place to go to and that was London.

*

London in the spring of 1949 was still showing plenty of the scars of her wartime wounds but to me she was the flower of cities all, after Leeds so feminine, sexy and glamorous that the mere thought of walking through her streets and parks was like the prospect of meeting with a new, very lovely and welcoming girl. The first sharp thrill of being in London was soon to be modified but it has never entirely disappeared. I rented a bed-sitter in Notting Hill Gate and began to look for work.

An employment agency put me in touch with an American publisher of, among other things, a trade magazine which needed someone to handle the layout of the advertisements. I was surprised to be given the job on the dubious grounds that I knew something about typography and layout since I had worked for a publisher, though the most cursory questioning would have uncovered my complete ignorance of printing and picture reproduction. Where I turned out to be extraordinarily lucky was in my 'assistant', a girl of about eighteen named Katherine who was perfectly capable of doing the job on her own, and I was perhaps even luckier in that she found the situation very funny and did not seem in the least to resent my nominal superiority and higher wage, even when in fact she found herself doing my job—with me as her almost wholly incompetent assistant.

The agencies or advertising departments of the various engineers and tool manufacturers who advertised in our pages would send us either copy or pictures from which blocks had to be made or in some cases, if the product were something small, a sample of the thing itself which we arranged to have photographed. My days at the office were punctuated by the ringing of the telephone and confident busy voices at the other end of the line rattling out some mumbo-jumbo like: 'That three-colour job for so-and-so's lathe, what kind of screen do you want me to use?' and I would say, 'Hold on a second, I'm on the other phone', cover the mouthpiece and repeat the meaningless question to Katherine and then relay her confident and informed reply to my questioner. Before each issue of the magazine was published we had to make up a 'dummy' of its advertising pages which far exceeded in number the space allotted for editorial matter. Again, it was Katherine who did all the work, and with her good-natured connivance I was able to hide my incompetence for the first couple of months or so. And then disaster fell. Katherine went on her summer holiday.

Without her at my side I was worse than useless. When the telephone rang I would pretend that I was from another department, that the man in charge was away sick and his assistant was on holiday. Then the time came for me to make up the dummy. I sat at my desk for hours with pot of paste, scissors and proofs of incomprehensible texts and pictures of lathes, turners, screws, bolts and anonymous lumps of metal that I supposed possessed some function hidden from me. Inevitably I made a mess of the job and, after the magazine had gone to press, I realized that at least one picture was going to be printed above the wrong caption and probably more than one of those photographs of mysterious metal objects would be reproduced upside down. It was time for me to leave. I walked out of the office and never went back. I hoped that the boss of the advertising department would have the sense to see that Katherine was the person for the job and that she was properly rewarded.

Of course I had not saved any money from the nine pounds a week I had been paid so I had to find fresh work at once. My next job was more within my range of abilities: I worked as dish-washer at one of the big hotels and it was while I was there that I finished a children's story which I sold outright for fifty pounds. I retired from dish-washing at once and decided to write a novel: I would discipline myself rigorously and force myself to get up early in the mornings putting in at least eight hours work each day. Allowing for free weekends I should be able to produce a good ten thousand words every week. At that rate the book would be finished in seven weeks, say two months at the outside. That meant that I had to live on six pounds a week which should not be too difficult. I had all the confidence of ignorance in my ability to write a novel though I had to admit that I was not too sure what the book was going to be about.

I was rescued from this problem by the unexpected arrival at my room one morning of my brother, Kenneth, who had been working on a farm in Hertfordshire since his wartime marriage had broken up shortly after his return from the Army to civilian life in 1946.

I told him about my good luck in selling the children's story and he said, 'That's marvellous news. Fifty quid will get us over to France and keep us quite a while there. Until we can get work picking grapes or something.'

At first I protested: I was going to write a novel; I was not at all sure I wanted to pick grapes in France. In any case why should I spend my money on a holiday for him?

'I'm not talking about a holiday,' he said. 'Look. You're what? Twenty-seven. I'm twenty-nine. This is our last chance. Europe's open to us. Most of the world's open. But if we don't go now we never will. We'll be too old, too timid, too tied up by habit and sloth. I'm not being romantic. I'm being realistic. If we don't grab this chance it'll never come again. We'll get rid of everything. Flog everything that'll raise a penny. Get a one-way ticket across the Channel and start moving south. Take a chance. What have we got to lose? A few quid that won't last you more than a couple of weeks or so anyway. Whatever happens, we'll survive.'

He saw that his enthusiasm was beginning to infect me. 'Think of it. The wine, so cheap they almost give it away. You wouldn't need much cash once you were in the south. Sleep out. Buy bread, wine, cheese, fruit for next to nothing. What more could you want?'

'I don't know,' I said doubtfully.

'Listen. You want to be a writer. Think of the material you'll get. And another language. You know a bit of French, don't you? Well, you'll soon be speaking it like a native after you've been over there a few months.'

I said, 'Have you got any money?'

'Not much but I'll get some. I've got one or two things I can sell. I've got a good camera and a watch. Then there's my records and books.'

'Books!' I was horrified. 'You mean you'd sell your books?'

'Yes. Why not? Possessions are a curse. They imprison you. If you don't sell everything it means you're hedging. You're not serious. You mean to come back, and soon.'

He saw that the prospect of losing my books was beginning to put the proposed adventure into a different and darker perspective so he said quickly, 'Maybe you're right though. You always get robbed when you sell books. We'll find somewhere to store them.'

'All right,' I said, 'I'm with you.'

During the next few days Kenneth stayed with me, sleeping at night on the floor, and we busied ourselves making arrangements for our emigration, first getting passports and then buying single train and boat tickets for Paris from where we would hitch-hike south. I persuaded a friend to give my books shelf-room and we bought cheap ex-army packs which were big enough to carry all the things we needed but were not so comfortable to wear as the more expensive rucksacks. After we had paid for our tickets we had between us just over forty-five pounds, all of which we changed into francs.

The morning of our departure was bright with excitement and sunshine as we rode on the top of a fifty-two bus to Victoria, watching the crowds of men and women on the pavements hurrying with strained and haunted faces to their shops and offices. We felt an olympian pity for them, poor slaves of convention who were so blinkered by habit and trammelled by their tiny bourgeois aspirations that they were unable to see, as we had seen, how simple it was to change the dull course of existence and redirect it into fresh and exciting territories. Our packs did not weigh heavily as we boarded the train for Newhaven.

Euphoria was not diminished after we had reached the Gare Saint-Lazare and managed to find our way on the Métro to the left bank where, in the Rue Monsieur le Prince, we took a room at the first hotel we saw. High above the narrow street we listened to the sounds of voices and traffic, savouring an experience we had never properly nown before because the only foreign travelling that either of us had done had been with the Army, and this was something altogether different.

We tidied ourselves up and left the hotel, deciding that we would not stint ourselves too severely on our first day abroad. We found a cheap restaurant where we ate salad, steak and fried potatoes and drank rough red wine. Then we found our way to the Boulevard Saint-Michel and sat outside a café in the warm night and drank more wine and watched the slowly moving parade on the pavement, smoked our Gauloises and listened to the lovely, incomprehensible chatter at the tables around us, incomprehensible because, although I had believed I understood French and could in fact read the language fairly well, I had never until then heard it properly spoken; it was disconcerting to realize that the sounds I made when I thought I was speaking French were related to the speech of the natives scarcely at all. Kenneth, to whom I had boasted of my knowledge of the language, was amused by my attempts to understand and be understood but his mockery was restrained since he could not attempt a single word.

At about midnight we returned to the hotel, slightly drunk and optimistic though vague about the future, certain that the French way of life was going to be very much to our taste. Before we fell asleep Kenneth said, 'We'll have to make plans to move on to-morrow.'

'Yes,' I said, 'we must.'

The next morning the unfamiliar music of the street and the sun slicing through the dimness of the room swung us quickly into full wakefulness. We got up, washed, shaved and dressed and went out and drank two large cups of *café au lait* each and ate a couple of *croissants*. Already the sun was quite hot.

Kenneth said, 'I suppose we ought to move on today.'

I supposed so too.

We each smoked a Gauloise.

He said, 'Of course, if we go south and maybe into Italy God knows when we'll see Paris again. Perhaps never. Seems a pity since we're here not to see a bit more of it. I think we could spare one day and move on tomorrow. What do you think?'

I agreed. Just one day. I was sure we could spare that.

So we walked to Notre Dame and climbed the tower and then had a look around the Louvre. We bought a loaf, cheese and tomatoes, a litre of the cheapest red wine and a couple of peaches and we ate and drank, sitting on a bench by the river. The sun grew hotter and when we had finished our meal we strolled along by the side of the Seine until we came to a *piscine*, one of those enclosed swimming-pools into which the river water is filtered.

Kenneth and I looked at each other. We both were hot and sweaty.

'What about it?' I said.

He nodded and we went to the entrance and hired bathing-slips and towels and were led into the place and allotted cabins for changing. The *piscine* was fairly crowded, mainly by young and beautiful people with skins of various shades of brown from lightly baked gold to rich mahogany. Kenneth and I emerged from our cabins and looked at one another with distaste, knowing that each was a mirror to the other. In that emphatic light we both looked unhealthily pale.

'Best thing we can do', Kenneth said, nodding at the water, 'is hide ourselves in there.'

He dived in and I followed him. We were both quite good swimmers and we soon forgot our miserable pallor as we exhausted ourselves in the water and then lay in the sun gazing with melancholy but pleasurable lust at the young women and with melancholy but less pleasurable envy at the young men.

That evening we ate in the same place as on the previous night and drank a good deal more wine.

'It's been a good day,' Kenneth said, not too distinctly, as we climbed into bed, 'but tomorrow we've got to hit the trail. Fun and games are over.'

The next day we went to the *piscine* again, as we did for the next four hot and golden days. Our skins were beginning to take on a respectable tan. Though we were rising in the mornings with hangovers we found that swimming and drowsing in the sun soon dispelled them and we were able to enjoy our food and drink in the evenings.

If the weather had not suddenly changed I believe we would have stayed in Paris until we were broke, but at the end of our first week we got up on a Sunday morning to find no welcoming sun but the long grey sigh of continuous rainfall. This had a sobering effect on us. We counted our money and found that we had spent over a quarter of our total wealth.

I said, 'We aren't going to last long at this rate.'

Kenneth looked resolute. 'As soon as this bloody rain stops we'll be on our way. We're acclimatized now.'

I agreed. 'Right. And we'd better keep a sharper eye on the money.'

'We will,' Kenneth said, 'we really will.'

We started economizing by not eating a cooked meal at all that day but by bringing bread and *pâté* and the cheapest wine that we could find into our hotel room. We ate and drank and watched the rain falling past the windows on to the deserted street below. When we finished the first litre of wine Kenneth volunteered to go out and fetch another.

'After all, it's so cheap it hardly matters.'

'Quite,' I said.

'Might as well get two.'

'Might just as well.'

So we spent that Sunday getting stewed, at first quietly and later, after the third or fourth expedition for more wine, more noisily, until we got bored by confinement and went to a little café and drank Pernod at the bar. The next morning neither of us remembered much about getting back to the hotel and we were both suffering from vicious hangovers. The rain had stopped but the sky was still bleak and watery. The day after that, we agreed, when our hangovers were reduced to manageable size, we would set out on the journey south. And rather surprisingly that is what we did.

*

We took a train to Etampes, a dispirited place dozing on a long yawn of a main street, and from there we started to walk. The weather was fine again and we sweated under the weight of our packs. We waved unpractised and self-conscious thumbs at the south-bound traffic as it whizzed, unheeding, past. We grew hotter, more tired and bad-tempered. Quite a few of the glossy cars that passed us had empty seats but none of the drivers seemed to notice us. We had almost given up all hope of a lift when a small and battered lorry stopped whose driver, as I managed to understand, was heading for Orleans. Gratefully we accepted his invitation to hop on the back.

We spent that night in Orleans and the next day we got a lift, again on a lorry, to Amboise. It was another hot day, and it was at this stage of our trip that my recollections become blurred and fragmentary because we were becoming more and more doped by heat and alcohol which wove a distorting veil of unreality over events, a sense of strangeness that was increased by our being in a foreign country, never fully communicating with people, often making wild misinterpretations that resulted in Alice-in-Wonderland dialogues and situations, and increased, too, by our being constantly on the move to a destination that became the more spectral and elusive the farther we travelled.

I think it was in Tours that Kenneth and I had a fight late at night in the central Place, cheered on by a big crowd of onlookers which included, I am sure, at least two policemen who were as enthusiastic as anybody. The next morning we were both bruised and marked around the face but neither of us could remember why we had fought—not that alcoholically stimulated fights between us were very rare events and it was not unusual to have no recollection of the cause of the conflict if, in fact, there were any cause beyond long-buried rivalries and jealousies of childhood or the hunger for competitive action and excitement.

I remember a little more about our stay in Poitiers because we were there for a couple of weeks or so. The weather was too hot for walking like mules under the weight of our packs; the sky was a Mediterranean blue and the sun banged its great gong from dawn to sunset and the air danced and sang to its tempo. We were given a very cheap room in a friendly hotel and we were told that there was a place to swim not far out of town. Each day we went there and lay in the sun and swigged our wine and, when we were too hot for comfort, we would plunge into the river and splash and wallow like drunken seals. In the evenings we ate in a plebeian restaurant with long scrubbed tables and benches. Great bowls of soup were placed before the diners who helped themselves to as much as they wanted, and for those with sufficiently robust appetites other courses followed: feathery omelettes, succulent fish, steaks, veal, cooked vegetables, fresh salads and fruit. The wine was cheap, harsh and potent. I have never, before or since, enjoyed food and drink so much.

Then one hungover morning we realized that, after settling the hotel bill, we would be almost broke. Our idyll had come to an end. We packed our rucksacks and spent our last few francs on a couple of litres of red anaesthetic.

When both bottles had been drained, we decided that the only thing to do was to try, without tickets, to get on a train to Paris and hope to avoid detection at the other end. Then we would go to the British Consulate and get ourselves repatriated. If we failed even to get on a train we would hand ourselves and our problems over to the local police. It was as well that we were pretty drunk or I doubt that we would have so simplified our circumstances and our plans or that we would have been as lucky as we proved to be, for there was a train to Paris stopping at Poitiers at midnight and we were able to get on to it, find a compartment to ourselves and sleep the anxious hours away until we drew into Paris the next morning.

Before we got off the train I said to Kenneth, 'We'll hang about a bit and then try and bluff our way through the barrier. Just say we're English, don't know any French, and let's hope they think we're mad or drunk.'

'They wouldn't be far wrong on both counts,' Kenneth grunted as he heaved his pack on to his back and squeezed out of the compartment.

There were so few passengers on the train that our appearance on the platform must have been observed by the ticket-collector, so there was no point in loitering. We walked purposefully to the barrier, staring ahead, past the official, as if he were invisible, but he was not to be ignored. He blocked our path and demanded our tickets. I tried to look amiably puzzled.

'What's he saying?' I asked Kenneth.

'Don't know.'

'We're English,' I said to the ticket-collector. 'English. Anglais. Don't speak French.'

He repeated, with some signs of impatience, his demand for our tickets.

We again said that we were English and did not know what he was talking about. He shouted over his shoulder and was joined by another railwayman. They conferred for a few seconds, then the second man left. We made another move to get past the barrier, but the ticket-collector again barred our way, looking fierce and shaking his head, telling us that we must wait. Then the second man returned with a third who was not in uniform.

The newcomer said, in more than adequate English, 'You must show your tickets.'

Our one flimsy shield, ignorance of the French language, had been flicked aside. I was flustered. 'I'm sorry. We can't. We've lost them. I mean I've lost them. I was looking after them both, you see, and I seem to have lost them.'

'Where have you come from?'

'Poitiers.'

'If you have no tickets you will have to pay the fares.'

'I'm afraid we can't. We haven't got any money.'

'You have no money, no money at all?'

He looked and sounded disbelieving.

'None at all.'

He said something rapidly to the man in uniform and then turned back to me. 'Are you quite sure you have lost the tickets? Perhaps you should look for them again.'

I pretended to search my pockets. 'No, it's no good. I know I've lost them.'

'What about your friend?'

Kenneth went through the act of searching himself. 'No good.'

I said, 'Look, we were drunk. We'd drunk a lot of stuff called Pern something—Pernos or Pernod—something like that.' My pronunciation was heavily anglicized.

'Pernod?'

'Yes, I think that was what they called it. You put a drop of water in it and it went sort of cloudy. It didn't taste very strong but I don't remember much about anything after we'd had a dozen or so.' I could tell by Kenneth's face that he thought I was overdoing it but I thought I now saw a line to take. 'You see, we bought our tickets in the morning so I suppose I could have lost them while I was drinking. Or perhaps they were stolen with my wallet. I certainly lost my wallet. That's why we've got no money. I was looking after all the money and the tickets.'

'Not very carefully,' he said, but his voice was less cold and I imagined there was a faint smile behind the words.

'It was that drink. It seemed so mild but it just about knocked us out. I can still taste it. I feel terrible.' This at least was true.

'If you have no money and no tickets what are you going to do? Have you lost your tickets to England also?'

'Everything. I had everything in my wallet.'

'Your passports?'

'No. We've got them in our packs.'

'That is fortunate.'

He again spoke to the ticket-collector, explaining that we were two crazy Englishmen who had drunk too much Pernod and lost all our money as well as our tickets. He said more, which I could not understand, and the uniformed man guffawed. Kenneth and I shuffled and looked oafish.

He turned back to us. 'You have been very foolish. You could have much trouble. It is a crime to travel on the railway without tickets. It is the same in other countries. You would not do it in England, would you? No. Then why do you do it in France?' He shook his head and seemed to ponder our case for a few seconds. Then he said, 'But we will let you go. You are very lucky that it is I and not some of my colleagues who would have you arrested. And in future you must be more careful and do not drink much Pernod. It is not like your English beer.'

We agreed that it was not in the least like our English beer.

He said, 'And where will you go now?'

I said, 'I thought perhaps the British Consulate might help us to get back.'

'Yes, that is the best place for you to go. I will tell you how to get there . . .'

We had, of course, no money for the Métro so we had to walk to the Consulate. It seemed a long time since we had been in Paris and we were both silently conscious of the difference between our first and second visits to the capital. The liveliness of the streets seemed now to be mocking or at least indifferent to our indigence and the foreignness which had formerly been excitingly exotic was now coldly alien and excluding. The heart of the city had turned to stone.

A couple of hours later we were interviewed by a middle-aged English lady who clearly did not feel much sympathy for our predicament.

'Why on earth didn't you get return tickets?' she said.

I explained, 'We didn't mean to go back. At least not for some time. We meant to get work over here, maybe move on into Italy.'

'What sort of work?'

'Well, anything. We thought we'd be able to pick grapes and then work on a farm or something. Maybe teach English.' I could hear, as I spoke, how feeble it sounded.

She flicked open one of our passports which lay on the desk in front of her. 'Pick grapes in early August?' she said. 'Didn't you even bother to find out when the harvest began? And haven't you any idea of the unemployment figures in France?'

We shuffled and mumbled and tried to avoid her look which was eloquent of disapproval and disbelief that such stupidity could exist.

'Wouldn't it have been a good idea to enquire about these things before you set out on this ridiculous enterprise?'

We felt like truant schoolchildren before a stern headmistress.

I sounded sulky: 'We'd heard of people who'd done it.'

Her lips tightened and I felt she would have liked to reach for the cane. 'You'd heard of people who'd picked grapes in August?'

'Well, no. I mean people who'd come over and lived for months and got odd jobs and managed to travel about and . . .' I shrugged '. . . you know.'

'Evidently more resourceful people than you two.'

'Evidently.'

She sighed. 'Well, since you're here, I suppose we'll have to get you home. You've no money at all, you say?'

We shook our heads.

'I don't suppose you've got spare passport photographs, have you?'

By good luck we had both kept the spare print from the three that we had had taken for our passports. We handed them over to her.

She said, 'That's a help anyway. It'll save some time. Now what happens is this. I want these pictures for the temporary documents that I'll have fixed up for you. You won't get your passports back until you've repaid the cost of your fares home. I'll advance you a few francs, too—a very few francs—so that you can get a sandwich or something. Now, if you'll wait outside I'll arrange for the documents to be prepared and you'll be given tickets from Saint-Lazare, via Dieppe to Victoria. And you must use the tickets. Today.'

When, after a long wait, we left the Consulate we each had a travel ticket and a buff form with the passport photograph fixed on to it and printed at the top in bold type the words: EXPATRIATED AT THE EXPENSE OF HIS MAJESTY'S GOVERNMENT. We had also been given the equivalent in francs of five shillings each. We walked away from the scene of our humiliation, each of us shrouded for the moment in the privacy of his shame, despondency and hangover.

At last, Kenneth said, 'We didn't show up too well in there.'

'No, we didn't. I thought she might have been a bit more human though.'

'You remember *Henry V*,' Kenneth said. 'That bit after the French have killed the boys. I thought I ought to say it to that old bird in there. You remember it? "I was not angry since I came to France until this instant." But I don't think she'd have been amused, somehow.'

I managed a token laugh, but it was hard work. The weight of failure and the uncertainty of the future were heavy upon us.

We crossed the Channel at night and arrived at Victoria at about six o'clock in the morning. We were tired, hungry and dishevelled and we had not a penny between us. London looked plainer, more familiar, but not much more welcoming than Paris.

Kenneth had a friend in Croydon who, he thought, could put him up until he had found a job.

'What about you?' he said. 'Where are you going to go?'

'Aylesbury's the only place I can think of.'

'You won't be very welcome there.'

'I know I won't,' I said, 'but I can't think of anywhere else.'

*

My mother and father had been divorced at the end of the war and she had moved from the small village near Princes Risborough, where they had been living for about three years, back to Aylesbury and a life of solitary and modest self-indulgence in a drab Victorian terrace house almost opposite the Bucks County Hospital. The appetites she indulged were innocent ones: a girlish greed for sweets and an uncritical taste for novels, swallowed with nearly the same speed as the chocolates and toffees she enjoyed so much. She had a few friends, most of them fellow-worshippers at the local Christian Science Church, but she was not a sociable woman, showing a distinct preference for the company of domestic animals to that of humans and I had no doubt that my own company would be unwelcome to her. She disapproved of alcohol, tobacco and sexual pleasure and held strongly to the belief that a man should work hard at a respectable occupation, behave always in a way that would frustrate scandal-mongers and arouse the envy of neighbours. Her two sons were a disappointment to her except that 'disappointment' seems too strong a word for the way that she nodded and sighed in an almost self-congratulatory style as if she could have long ago predicted our various failures in love, work and social advancement.

When I arrived with my pack on my back, dirty, unshaven and desperately tired and hungry she sighed and nodded in the familiar way and asked me how long I intended to stay.

I said, 'I won't stay long. Just a few days until I get a job.'

'And what have you done this time?'

I told her that I had been to France, but the job over there that

119

I had been promised had not materialized and I was temporarily without money and work.

She nodded again. 'And where are you thinking of looking for a job? Around here?'

I reassured her quickly. 'No. In London. I'll watch the papers every day. Something's bound to show up soon. I'll take anything to be going on with.'

Her smile was thin and sceptical.

I bathed and shaved and ate a tantalizingly small meal. Many foods were still rationed at this time and I knew better than to ask for more supper though I had already given my mother my ration book which had in it enough unused coupons to make her eyes gleam.

During the next few days I would go each morning to the reading-room of the public library and go through the Situations Vacant columns of *The Times* and the *Daily Telegraph* and copy down details of any job that I thought I might be capable of performing. I applied for at least a dozen vacancies, from assistant in a newspaper reference library to porter at a big block of flats but most of my letters went unanswered and the only offer of a job that I received was from the publishers of a children's encyclopaedia who were willing to appoint me as a sales representative, which meant going from door to door trying to persuade simple-minded housewives to buy the shoddy publication. When I asked what the wages were the smooth sales-manager blandly told me that his reps preferred to work on commission, which was very high, since they could earn far more than on a fixed salary. In other words, there was no wage at all.

My mother lent me a few shillings for tobacco, but that was all. Apart from being troubled by an uneasy awareness of her disapproval and resentment of my presence I was not unhappy there: I took advantage of the chance to do some solid reading and I managed to write two or three quite readable poems. Then I came across an advertisement in *The Times* inviting teachers of all subjects who were interested in working in the London area to write to a box number sending details of experience. There was something about the tone of the advertisement that suggested that I might not be wasting my time in applying: for one thing the usual 'Graduate' or

'Qualified' that prefixes 'Teacher' in most announcements of vacant appointments had been omitted and there was something vague about the general wording of the thing that gave me the idea that the advertiser might not be too fussy about academic qualifications. I wrote off, saying that I had been educated at Leeds University—without mentioning that I had not taken a degree there—and that I had taught in a prep school in Yorkshire. The subjects I offered were English and history, the stand-bys, as I suspected, of the formally uneducated.

Towards that weekend I felt unusually restless. I had not had a drink for about a fortnight and the strain of living under the tacitly begrudging patronage of my mother was beginning to fret at my nerves. I had not looked up any of my old friends, partly because I could not have paid for a drink if, as would almost certainly have been the case, we had celebrated our reunion in a pub; and partly because I guessed that I would find, like most people who have not seen an acquaintance for a number of years, we would meet as strangers, sharing only vague memories of the youngsters we once had been. But, early on a Saturday evening, my edginess and boredom forced me out of the house and into the town and I was walking down the High Street when a tall, strongly-built young man stopped me.

'It's Vernon, isn't it?' he said.

I did not recognize him immediately.

Then I said, 'Good God! Eddie MacSweeney!'

We had been close friends at school but had seen less of each other once we had gone out to work and nothing at all since the outbreak of war when Eddie, as a Territorial, had been instantly called to the colours and sent off to Northern Ireland where, it appeared, he had spent his entire military service in tedious safety. As a schoolboy he had been undersized, mischievous almost to the point of delinquency, quick and unpredictable like an intelligent monkey. Now he had the build of a heavyweight but I could just see a trace of the wicked urchin face almost concealed behind the meaty mask of maturity.

He said, 'Come and have a drink.'

'I can't. I'm broke. Absolutely flat.'

'I didn't ask you for money. I asked you to come and have a drink. So come on.'

I went.

An hour and two or three pints later he said, 'Still do any boxing?'

'Not for a couple of years.'

I saw that he was not asking without reason. 'Why? What makes you ask?'

He grinned. 'You said you were broke.'

'Well?'

'There's a fair on. They've got a boxing booth. Why don't you have a go? You might pick up a few quid.'

'No,' I said. 'Impossible. I haven't had the gloves on for ages. I wouldn't go more than three rounds.'

'You wouldn't have to. I've seen 'em. I was there last night. Honest, you could lick the lot of them put together. Listen. It's not eight o'clock yet. Let's have another drink and then we'll go along and have a look. I've got the bike parked in the Square. It won't take us a minute.'

'The bike?'

'Yeah. Ariel five hundred. Drink up.'

Twenty minutes later we were dismounting at the entrance to the fairground. The beer, after my period of abstinence, had made me just a little drunk. Rationally, I knew that going into the ring, whatever the quality of the opposition, was not a good idea, but the beer had awakened another, cheerfully optimistic part of me, and I knew that it was this part that was going to take over and dictate my actions that night. The noise of the fair, the doctored rifles cracking like little whips at the shooting galleries, the pounding rhythms of the hurdy-gurdy music, the impotent plonks of the wooden balls on iron coco-nuts, the screams of delighted terror from the chair-o'planes, all fed my sense of irresponsible happiness.

I said, 'Where's the boxing booth then?'

'This way. Over there, look.'

We saw it before we were close enough to hear what the barker was bawling into his microphone. The ornate façade at the front of the marquee was exactly as I remembered it from childhood, a flimsy structure beaded with small electric light bulbs framing the stage in front of the booth and decorated with crude pictures of ancient fighters doing battle and the words: *Alf Taylor's Boxing Academy.*

Alf Taylor was a small man but he had a big voice which was now reaching us clearly through the din of the fairground. In the hand that was not holding the microphone he brandished a fearsome-looking sword. Behind him, looking bored and impassive, were four boxers, all of them wearing shabby robes and towels round their necks. Occasionally one or other of them would give a little shuffle and subdued dance and throw a couple of lethargic jabs or hooks into the air, but for the most part they stood still staring glumly out above the heads of the crowd.

We pushed our way to the front of the gathered spectators. I knew enough about boxing booths to realize that they always had one of their own men, known as a 'gee', planted in the audience, ready to come forward and challenge one of the resident fighters. This was a sensible precaution to take since legitimate challengers were few and, if none was to come forward, the show could hardly go on. Now that I had decided to have a go I did not want to be frustrated by having the 'gee' answer the barker's invitation before I could get there.

Mr Taylor was in full spate: 'All right then!' he yelled. 'I think we're going to see some action tonight, some real old-fashioned fighting like you never see in the posh halls. No quarter asked and no quarter given. Anybody among you good folk what thinks he can fight can take his pick from my boys up here.' He pointed with his sword. 'First, Johnny Batsford, ex-contender for the Southern Area Featherweight Title. Step forward, Johnny, and let these lovely people have a look at you.'

The smallest of the four boxers stepped forward, waved to the crowd and shuffled round the small stage shadow-boxing before returning to his place. He was very pale, a thin hard face with black hair well-greased and centre-parted in the style of the thirties, shining like a guardsman's toe-caps, a bent nose and scar tissue above both eyes.

Alf Taylor went on: 'If you fancy something a bit bigger, we've got Mick Daly at welter, weighing ten stone seven pound, and Harry Fay at eleven stone six. Step forward Mick and Harry.'

The middleweight, Harry Fay, was the one who interested me. He looked as if he had taken plenty of beatings over a long and undistinguished career and I saw that the cropped hair above his cauliflower ears was beginning to go grey.

'And if you really want to make a meal of it,' the barker continued, 'we've got Pete Sloman of the United States of America and he tips the scales at fourteen stone. You can take your pick. Anyone lasting eight rounds with any one of these boys gets five pound. If he can stop our boy inside the distance he gets ten pound . . . Now, who's going to step up then? . . . Come on, there must be some local lad what can use his mitts. Let's see what Aylesbury lads are made of. I've heard of Aylesbury duck, but don't tell me you're all chicken!' He gave a sharp yelp of laughter.

I guessed that the 'gee' would be stepping up at any moment so I mounted the steps that led to the stage.

'Hello-hello!' he said. 'What have we got here then? Here's your local challenger, folks. What's your name, son?'

'Smart,' I said, still not entirely sober.

'Smart, eh? What's your first name?'

'Kit.'

'What's that? Kid? Kid Smart. Okay. Here you are then, folks, your local fighter, Kid Smart from Aylesbury. Let's hope he's a smart 'un with his mitts. All right, Kid Smart, which one of my boys do you fancy yourself against?'

I said I would take the middleweight.

'Right. That's Harry Fay. Now listen, folks, Kid Smart of Aylesbury is going to fight Harry Fay over eight rounds. He's going to go in there and try and win himself ten pound by knocking out my lad inside eight rounds. If he can't win by a kayo but goes the distance, he gets a fiver.' He turned to me and said, off-mike, 'You got any gear? . . . You haven't? That's okay. Pete'll fix you up. Go round with him to the caravan at the back, get changed and come back up here.'

I left the stage with Pete Sloman of the United States and we went to the large caravan at the back of the booth. Inside, he said in the unmistakable accents of Birmingham, England, 'What size boots you take, mate?'

'Nines.'

'These'll do. Bit big but that's better than too small. Here you are, here's a pair of trunks. Haven't got a dressing-gown for you but you can borrow this coat if you like. I would if I was you. It's bloody nippy out there.'

I thanked him and when I had changed I draped the old army greatcoat over my shoulders and went back with him on to the stage where Alf was demonstrating the steeliness of Mick Daly's nerves by making vigorous passes with his sword quite close to the boxer's nose. I hoped that he would not expect me to undergo a similar test. Up there in the cold autumnal night air, feeling the sniping curiosity and mockery of the crowd, my alcoholic self-confidence drained rapidly away and I began to wonder what I had let myself in for.

Alf shouted into his microphone, 'Here's your local boy, folks! Here's Kid Smart. He looks in good shape, so I hope we're going to see a real fight.' He turned to me and said, still into the mike, 'Can you fight? Come on, tell these good people, Can you fight?' Then he thrust the instrument in front of my face for my reply.

I muttered that I hoped so, and from the crowd's laughter I guessed that I sounded as coy as a young girl at her first dance.

Alf snarled into the mike, 'He says he can fight. Well, we'll see. We'll see whether he can fight or not when he gets up there in the ring with my boy, Harry Fay. We'll see whether Kid Smart's a smart 'un or not. Because, if he aint, he won't last long in there with Harry 'cos Harry's fought some of the best in the business.' Then, in such contrast to his snarling, leather-lunged ferocity that, for a second, I was bewildered, he muttered to me, off-mike: 'You boxed in a booth before, son? You haven't, have you? Well, listen. You take a dive in the sixth. Got it? A dive in the sixth.' Then once more he roared into his instrument: 'Roll up! Roll up! The pay-box is about to open. If you want to see a fight, and I mean a real fight, roll up and see Kid Smart of Aylesbury against Harry Fay of Bethnal Green over eight rounds.'

Pete was at my side. 'Come on, mate. Inside and up in the ring.'

I followed him into the marquee and climbed into the ring. Harry Fay was already in the opposite corner. Alf came into the ring with a set of very old and beat-up gloves and he tossed one pair to Pete and the other to Mick Daly who was acting as Fay's second. Pete laced my gloves on. Alf, who was acting as both master of ceremonies and referee, made a great show of the introductions and the centre-of-the-ring instructions before sending us back to our corners. As I waited for the start of the fight I began to feel the familiar tension, the mixture of anticipation and apprehension. I had no intention of taking a dive. If I were capable of it I was going to knock Harry Fay out and win myself ten pounds.

Johnny Batsford, who was acting as time-keeper, shouted, 'Seconds out of the ring . . . first round . . .' and he hit the gong.

I moved out briskly and jabbed with three or four lefts, finding the target quite easily and, as Fay threw a swinging left hook, I slipped inside it with a short right and hit him on the chin. He almost went down but managed to recover and start back-pedalling. I thought, 'This is going to be easy.' If Harry Fay had ever been any good, which I very much doubted, he was certainly past it now.

I took my time, jabbing with the left, moving it from head to body and back again, keeping him from getting in close which was obviously his dearest wish. I feinted with the left, then let it go through and I saw an opening, banged over the right and, as he staggered back to the ropes, his eyes rolling, the gong sounded for what must have been the shortest round in the history of boxing. Alf waved me back to my corner and when I was on my stool I said to Pete, who was flapping a towel ineffectually in front of my face, 'How long are the rounds supposed to be?'

He stopped waving the towel. 'That's up to Alf. He gives Johnny the wink when to hit the gong.'

I was surprised that the crowd had not noticed the absurdly short round but then I remembered that booth patrons are unlike the crowds you get at proper professional shows: they are, on the whole, ignorant of the game, only there for a bit of fun and excitement. Nowadays, since so much good-class boxing is shown on television, I imagine that spectators would not be so easily taken in.

The second round began with a flurry of action from Harry who rushed from his corner, swinging wildly and hoping to catch me with a sucker punch. I moved back to the ropes and almost fell through them, they were so slack, but I evaded his attack and began to get the left working again. I thought that if I could get another crack at his chin I would make sure that he would go down and stay down and there would be nothing Alf could do except hand over my ten pounds.

Harry had apparently given up all aggressive intentions and was moving backwards, ready to cover up at the first sign of real trouble. He was not much of a boxer but he had been around long enough to make it difficult to catch him properly when he was intent only on survival. After about a minute of the round, however, I got through with a hard left hook to the solar-plexus and Harry dropped to his knees, rolled over on his side, groaning loudly, and clutched his balls.

Alf yelled, 'Stop!' and went across to see how poor Harry was faring. He helped him to his feet, taking his time about it. 'Can you box on?' he said.

Harry groaned, declining to commit himself.

Alf turned to me. 'That was a low punch. This is a final warning. Keep 'em up or I'll toss you out of the ring. Understand? One more like that and you'll be disqualified.'

I started to protest. 'It was a good punch. It wasn't—' but he shouted me down: 'Don't argue with the referee. Box on!'

About twenty seconds later the gong sounded to end a slightly longer round that the first.

In my corner Pete said, 'You're being a bit naughty. You'll never get away with it. We know you could lick Harry with one hand tied behind your back, but it's Alf Taylor you've got to beat. Cleverer blokes than you have tried it.'

And he was right. In round three, when I caught Harry with a right to the chin Alf shouted, 'Stop!' and spent a good ten seconds warning Mick, Harry's second, that he must not give his man advice while the round was in progress. When we were told to box on Harry had recovered enough to slip a left lead and get into a clinch where he hung on like a drowning man. He soon showed me that he knew one or two rough tricks at close quarters and he managed to rattle my teeth when he brought his head sharply up under my chin. When I went back to my corner I knew I was tiring and I could taste regurgitated beer in my throat. I knew it had to be the next round.

I started fast and landed a couple of good jabs but he got underneath the third and, once again, grabbed me in a clinch. He trapped my right glove firmly under his left arm and, before I could free myself and push him away, he managed to get his own right glove to my face, palming upwards with the inside and the lace. I wrestled free, even more determined to finish him off after this blatant infringement of the rules. I stalked him to the ropes when Alf shouted, 'Stop! Stop boxing!'

I dropped my hands and turned to him in exasperation wondering what on earth he could be up to now. I soon found out. He came close, pushed my head back and peered into my face.

'Chuck us a towel, Mick,' he called.

Mick jumped on to the ring apron and handed his boss a grubby towel which Alf applied roughly to my face. It was rubbed hard over my brow and I thought I felt a slight pricking over my left eye.

'It's not a bad cut, son,' he said in a fatherly voice, 'but we can't let you go on. Not worth the risk. Back to your corner . . .' He turned to the crowd: 'Kid Smart has sustained a cut over his left eye and has to retire. We can't endanger a game boy's eyesight. I know it's a big disappointment to us all and to Harry Fay who was just beginning to warm . . .' the rest of his spiel was drowned in the boos from the thwarted spectators. He waved his arms, appealing for a hearing. Then he beckoned to me to join him in the middle of the ring. His hand went to his hip pocket and came out holding two pound notes.

'Ladies and gentlemen! Ladies and gentlemen! One moment please!' The booing subsided. 'I know you'll all agree Kid Smart put up a fine show in there and though the management is not obliged to offer any money I would like to give him, from my own pocket, a little something to show my appreciation of his performance here tonight. And I am sure you will show your own appreciation of a game lad when the cap comes round. Thank you. Thank you.' There was some applause and a few derisive hoots and whistles as Alf handed me the two pounds.

I went back to my corner where Pete was grinning widely. 'Told you you couldn't lick Alf, mate. Here you are, here's cap. Go round and get your nobbins before the buggers escape. You'll do well. The crowd was with you all the way. They'll dig deep.'

I looked at the greasy old cap he had pushed into my hand and wondered if I had sunk so low as to beg, cap literally in hand. I had. I went round the marquee with Harry Fay at my side and, as Pete had predicted, nearly everyone dropped silver coins into the cap. Then Harry, Pete and I left the booth and went into the caravan. There was a man I had not seen before sitting on one of the bunks. He wore a corduroy cap and, beneath the peak, his slightly sunken eyes and flattened nose advertised his profession. He nodded to me and said, 'Get good nobbins?'

Harry answered for me. 'We'll soon see.' He reached out to take the cap from me.

I drew it out of his reach. 'What's the idea?' I said, trying to sound more belligerent than I felt and wondering if I was now going to be punished for refusing to take a dive.

'Let's see how much we've got,' Harry said quite mildly.

'What do you mean "we"?'

'You always share nobbins. Anybody'll tell you.'

Pete said, 'That's right, mate. No kidding. You always share nobbins with the bloke you fight.'

'That's right,' said the man in the corduroy cap.

I could sense that they were telling the truth. 'Okay then,' I said and poured the coins on to one of the bunks and left Harry to divide them into two piles while I got dressed.

'Four pounds eighteen and seven,' Harry said. 'Not bad at all. That's two pound nine and—here you are kiddo. Make it two pound ten.'

As I was pocketing the load of coins Alf came into the caravan. He stood in the doorway, looking at me with a faint grin and nodding to himself. Then he said, 'You're a right bugger, you are. Kid Smart, eh? But not quite smart enough. Thought you'd catch me for a tenner but you couldn't kid the kid who's kidded millions. Still, I admit you gave me a couple of anxious moments in there. I thought you was going to knock that silly old sod's head off.' He laughed. 'Did you feel me scratch you? Under the towel? That was me thumbnail. Just enough to get a spot of blood. Clever, eh?'

'Very clever.'

'All right, son, don't take it to heart. You've earned yourself a few quid without raising a sweat. And listen. If you play along with us and do what you're told you could pick up a lot more. High Wycombe's our next pitch. You come along with us and play the gee there and I'll see you're all right. But no coming the wide-o this time. If it's your turn to take a dive, you take a bloody dive. Right? If you take a dive the first time, we fix a return for the next night, see? That gets the crowds in. They want to see you get your own back. Next time, the other fella takes the dive. Okay, so you have a decider. The silly buggers fall over each other to get in and see it. I'll tell you this, son. You move good, you look good. A touch of class. We'd be glad to have you along, wouldn't we, boys?'

I was surprised at their friendliness. I had expected at least surliness if not much worse for having refused to obey Alf's instructions to go down in the sixth and for trying to knock his man out. I said I would probably go over to High Wycombe the following week.

'Well, let us know not later than teatime on Wednesday if you're going to be there or not. If you're not there by then we'll fix another gee. Arthur there', he said, nodding at the man in the corduroy cap, 'was the gee tonight but you beat him to it.'

'Yeah, I was too far back,' Arthur said. 'Didn't expect nobody to challenge like.'

I said goodnight and joined Eddie who was waiting outside.

He said, 'I was worried. I thought they might do you up when they got you back there.'

I told him that they had been very friendly.

'But what happened? Let's have a look at your eye. It doesn't look much.'

'It isn't much. I got rubbed with the lace in a clinch, just a little graze. You saw the referee stop us to have a look at it? He got the towel as if he was wiping a wound but what he did was scratch the graze with his thumbnail to get a spot of blood.'

'What a crook!'

I said, 'I'm easy. I got over four quid with the nobbins and I wasn't in there more than ten minutes. Let's go and have a drink before they close.'

We went and had a drink.

*

I boxed, or rather acted, three times at High Wycombe, rehearsing the evening performance each afternoon. I learnt how to drop my guard at a given signal from my opponent and ride with his open-gloved slap on the jaw which made a tremendous noise and caused the crowd to gasp and roar but was almost entirely painless and which sent me toppling to the canvas where, after the count of five, I would struggle valiantly to my knees only to keel over and be counted out. I also learnt how to deliver a fast, slack-fisted right-cross which I pulled at the last second so that, though it looked impressive, it carried no more weight than the merest flick and from this Harry would crash to the canvas when it was his turn to be counted out. I remembered reading in E. M. Forster's *Where Angels Fear to Tread* the splendid description of a small-town operatic production which, as he says, aimed not at illusion but at entertainment, and I thought the boxing booth went one better by offering both.

Alf paid me two pounds for each appearance and I was quite satisfied, but my career as boxing illusionist was soon to come to an end. I received an answer to my application for the teaching job from an address in the City of London inviting me to attend for an interview on the next Monday afternoon. The letter was signed by the Director of Education for a group of independent schools owned by a single profit-making organization. The function of these schools was to supply a better, or more ambitious, education than the Secondary Modern Schools offered to children who had failed to qualify for places in Grammar Schools and whose parents, while unable to afford the fees demanded by the public schools, were willing to pay more modest charges for more modest benefits and perhaps gain some prestige in the eyes of neighbours whose sons and daughters did not wear posh uniforms or study a foreign language.

I had sent a copy of a glowing if unmerited testimonial from

George Wilson Knight, and at the interview I explained that I had not taken a degree because, after five years of institutional life in the Army, I had felt that I was too old to spend a further three years at a University and I wanted to assert my independence and earn my living as soon as possible. I was told that there was a vacancy for a teacher of English and history at one of their schools in a West London suburb and they offered a salary of six pounds a week, acknowledging that this was not a large income but assuring me that the opportunities for advancement were unlimited. I accepted the job and agreed to start after half-term in a fortnight's time.

I returned to Aylesbury to pack and borrow ten pounds from my mother, and then I went back to London to rent a furnished basement room on Campden Hill near Notting Hill Gate. I collected my books from the man who had been looking after them and I settled down to enjoy two weeks of leisurely reading and writing before my new job began.

NOW

No ONE is the same person from cradle to grave. We change, apart from in the obvious physical ways. Habits of various kinds are gradually discarded while others take their place, habits of eating and drinking, habits of work and play, of thinking, feeling and speaking. All this is part of the process of ageing. I am not the person I was when I moved into the Campden Hill basement room twenty years ago, if only because I am a little more prudent, a little less hopeful and a lot closer to the end. Also I am the father of five children, and this alone makes of that young man who carried my name a person with whom I would now have less in common than with far more recent and not especially close acquaintances whose domestic circumstances are similar to my own. I have heard people speak of the delusion of change, but I think it would be closer to truth to speak of the delusion of unchange, the delusion that traps so many middle-aged or elderly people into situations that are grotesque, pathetic or embarrassing, the delusion that though you may be a bit short of breath and hair, a little thicker round the waist or sagging in the tits, you are still essentially the same person as the young man or woman of ten, twenty or thirty years ago. And yet the paradoxical fact remains that each one of us is himself and no one else and the sense of a continuous, unified and unique identity persists.

These vague speculations have been prompted by a visit by a journalist from the *Guardian* who is to write a piece about me for his newspaper. We talked for quite a long time, between two and three hours I suppose, and our conversation was taken down on his tape-recorder. He will make up his verbal portrait from my answers to his questions and I am sure that there will be no deliberate distortion, but I am equally sure that the picture that emerges will not have more than a superficial resemblance to the man my wife and closer friends believe they know. Nor to the man I sometimes think I know.

Introspective self-analysis is not only boring for other people to witness but it will be inevitably unproductive of the truth, for I do not believe that much self-knowledge is accessible to the conscious and self-conscious probings of rational instruments alone. I also believe that one of the functions of language used poetically is that it can explore experiences and the hidden sources of behaviour in a way that will not be tedious to the reader of the finished artefact, and since the goal of knowledge, secondary to the making of the poem, is forgotten in the excitement and rigours of the game or battle with words and shapes, self-interest is mislaid and objective truth may often be revealed. My admiration for and enjoyment of Freud are occasioned by Freud the poet, the man who thought in images, who saw and felt the illuminating power of riddles and puns, who saw beyond the verbal metaphor and the semantic explosion to the actual physical metaphors and puns of human behaviour.

Uneasily then I come back to the question of why I am writing this book instead of working on poems and I can only say that, as a writer, I must keep writing; poems can never be forced, the muses will not be raped, so I feel this kind of prose, which does, however inadequately, share some of the exploratory features of the poetic use of language, is the next best thing. I recognize, too, that the audience for poetry is not large and I hope that the free-ranging, anecdotal manner of this kind of writing might engage the interest of readers from whom I would otherwise be cut off. I am aware of the dangers of dredging too often and too deep into the past. The practice is another of the habits we pick up as we grow older, though some people are more given to it than others and I know that I am attracted temperamentally by the seductive and emasculating pleasures of nostalgia. This is not because I deceive myself that the past was, for me, a happier time: I know otherwise. It is not that I hanker for the physical and metaphysical advantages of youth, but rather because I believe that clues which might lead to the resolution of present problems and the amelioration of present predicaments are hidden somewhere in the darkening places of the past and, though they may never be discovered, the search is charged with the excitement of the possibility of their discovery. Yet, as soon as I have said this I begin to wonder whether I am rationalizing and trying to make respectable less honourable motives; to disguise a retreat from a present with which I cannot come wholly to terms, indulging myself in a re-shaping of events from which I, too, will emerge re-shaped and, of course, much improved. I am not sure. All I can do is go on, or rather go back, taking the present back into the past and bringing the past into the present, hoping that a coherence, a consolatory wholeness might at least be adumbrated.

THEN

MY BASEMENT room in Notting Hill smelled of dead cats and its furnishings were simple: a table, two upright chairs, an armchair and a divan bed. There was a gas fire and a ring, like an old rusted doughnut, for cooking on. I shared a bathroom with the occupants of the flat on the first floor. Hot water came from an ancient gas geyser which, after the pilot light had been lit and the tap turned on, would, more often than not, terrify you with a tremendous explosion and then you had to start all over again. I felt that I had earned a decoration for bravery every time I had a bath.

Notting Hill Gate was not a bad place to live in. I used the public library in Kensington High Street and there were second-hand bookshops to be explored, in one of which I picked up Auden's *Another Time*, Hardy's *Winter Words*, and the shorter poems of Matthew Prior for less than ten shillings the lot. There was also an interesting selection of pubs to be sampled when one was in the money. The one which was the nearest was, to my taste, very far from the best. The bars seemed more like film-sets for an English movie than the real thing and they were used mainly by a bunch of loud-voiced people who looked and sounded expensive. I thought at the time they might have been professionally connected with films, advertising or the better paid kind of journalism, but I now suspect that most of them were engaged in more humdrum occupations from which they were escaping into this vaguely theatrical ambience on their free evenings and weekends. A couple of years after I had left the district I returned one evening and was walking up Campden Hill Road when I bumped into Roy Campbell, whom I knew slightly, and we went into this particular pub since it was only a few yards away. Neither of us was drunk nor behaving in a noticeably eccentric manner but the barman, acting on the landlady's instructions, refused to serve us. We were very annoyed at the time but I have since felt, looking back at those plummy-voiced stuffed shirts and their whinnying mares of wives and girl-friends, that we were paid a decided compliment.

In Kensington Church Street was a more congenial pub frequented a good deal by painters (though this too was presided over by a rather disagreeable lady), and farther on towards the High Street, next door to and almost indistinguishable from an undertaker's, was a biggish anonymous kind of bar where I was once fed double scotches by a drunken Glaswegian tart who, for some reason, thought I was Polish and would not be persuaded otherwise. Not far away from Notting Hill Gate Underground Station was a big flashy pub where you often saw almost well-known stage and screen performers, many of them slightly and indefinably disreputable, the sort of comedian who was remembered, usually apocryphally, for having been barred by the BBC for telling dirty jokes over the air, or the kind of actor you were almost sure you had seen in a B film that you could not put a title to. A famous ex-boxer and singer often used the place and he seemed to embody the quality that characterized the atmosphere, making it both attractive yet depressing, a sense of tarnished gilt, a frayed flamboyance, a fearful but gay balancing on the edge of utter failure, neglect and derision. This man, with his dark pin-stripe suit that was beginning to shine and bag but never without a carnation in the buttonhole, his familiar, once-famous face sinking back into the anonymity of excess fat and public indifference, his off-white, slightly crumpled shirt collar, the listing heels of cracked shoes, he was there as the representative of the majority and a warning to the minority, who were still relatively prosperous and successful, of what lay in store for them unless they were very lucky.

Then there was The Prince Albert, where I played bar billiards, and a pub whose name I have forgotten, which stood facing the turning off Holland Park Road into Campden Hill Road, where I played darts with an Irishman from Shepherd's Bush who did no work because his wife kept him in enviable affluence, with the money she made as a prostitute. At the other end of Church Street was The

Catherine Wheel where my brother and I enjoyed a happy encounter with a stranger.

Kenneth was staying with me for the weekend and on the Saturday evening we went into the bar and decided that we would play a game which we often played for drinks and which we called *Quoting*. It was quite simple. One of us would recite at least four lines of verse and the other had to identify the author. If he failed he had to buy the drinks. Then it was his turn to supply the quotation and his partner's to give the poet's name.

We had played two or three rounds when we were approached by a man who had been standing near us at the bar. He was tall, dressed in the fashion of an old-type Guards officer in mufti, or perhaps a foreign office diplomat, or perhaps I mean a stage version of either; dark suit, impeccably white collar and discreetly distinguished tie. He carried an umbrella and bowler hat and looked expensively barbered and fed.

He said, 'Excuse me, gentlemen. I couldn't help overhearing you playing your game. Quite fascinating. I wonder if you'd mind terribly if I joined in.'

We were both startled but intrigued. 'Of course not,' we said.

Kenneth quoted something fairly simple: I think it was the Wordsworth lines from *Resolution and Independence*:

> My former thoughts returned: the fear that kills;
> And hope that is unwilling to be fed;
> Cold, pain, and labour, and all fleshly ills,
> And Mighty Poets in their misery dead.

Our new playmate shook his head. 'Splendid stuff,' he said, 'but I must confess I've no idea who wrote it.'

I gave the author's name, so he cheerfully bought a round of drinks.

Then it was his turn to quote. In a voice quite different from the one he used for conversation, in a higher key and rather parsonical in tone, he began:

> When I was one-and-twenty
> I heard a wise man say—

but he got no farther.

Kenneth and I chimed together: 'Housman!'

He looked both surprised and delighted. 'Right!' he said. 'What is it to be? I must say you chaps are pretty hot stuff at this game.' He provided another round of drinks and the game continued. When it was his turn to quote again he started to intone:

> Into my heart an air that kills
> From yon far country blows.
> What are—

'Housman!' we broke in with one voice.

Again, and with evident pleasure, he bought another round of drinks. We carried on playing. Our new friend failed to identify a single quotation from either of us and every time it was his turn to supply one he came up with lines from a Housman poem. It was obvious that he knew the collected works of A. E. Housman by heart but, it seemed, not a line of any other poet. He must have bought a dozen consecutive rounds of drinks and not once did he fail to register surprise at our acuity in spotting the authorship of his quotations nor did the alacrity with which he bought our drinks falter for an instant. In the closing stages of the game and the evening, Kenneth and I were slurring out ''oushman!' almost before the poor man had begun to quote and I am sure that if he had given us the most familiar lines from any other author—'To be or not to be' for instance—Kenneth and I would still have chorused ''oushman!'

But there were other, more austere delights in Notting Hill Gate than pubs. I had begun teaching and I found that the routine of a regular job helped me to impose some kind of order on my spare time. I worked hard, writing much that was feeble or confused, but now and then producing a few respectable lines and even an occasional poem that gave me the satisfaction of knowing that I had done something that was at least honest and reasonably well made. I sold a few poems to weeklies, the *Listener*, the *Spectator* and *Time and Tide* (which then had John Betjeman as its Literary Editor), and others appeared in those sometimes absurd but usually likeable little magazines like Wrey Gardiner's *Poetry Quarterly* and Dannie Abse's *Poetry and Poverty*. I was reading, too, with the kind of appetite and stamina which have long since declined, not only poetry, criticism and fiction, but psychology, biography and the history which, apart from the pleasure it offered, was now urgently necessary since I was teaching the subject along with English and, improbably, religious knowledge.

The school was an extraordinary place. Both boys and girls attended from the ages of twelve to about seventeen and their academic goal—rarely achieved and in few subjects—was the fairly new General Certificate of Education, Ordinary Level. The Headmaster was genial and kind-hearted with the appearance and manner of a failed music hall comedian and a touch of the not very successful con man. One afternoon each week the school played games in a nearby public park and the Headmaster, who was a soccer fan, would often referee one of the senior games. It was a memorable sight to watch him, whistle between teeth, Anthony Eden black hat firmly wedged on his head, the tails of his dark, businessman's coat flapping round his pin-striped legs and above his muddy football boots as he pounded up and down the field of play.

During the two years that I worked at the school I saw more teachers come and go than I can now remember: only those who themselves were remarkable, or whose circumstances of leaving were especially bizarre, have remained in the memory. One young man, who taught mathematics, aged a good ten years in a single term before he was carried away in a state of total nervous collapse induced not only by the recalcitrance of most of his pupils but by the zany inefficiency of the whole establishment. He was timid, sensitive and conscientious, a combination of attributes that was bound to condemn him to a painful and short-lived career at this institution.

Arthur Vivian Burberry joined the staff in my first spring term. He was a massive, very handsome man of about sixty who had been decorated for gallantry as a pilot in the Royal Flying Corps during the First World War, and was a more than competent classicist who commanded with complete authority a number of modern languages including Russian, Italian, French, Spanish and German. At some time he had published poetry and at least one novel. There had to be a snag. Men with the abilities and qualifications of Burberry did not work for six pounds a week in schools which had failed to gain

Ministry of Education recognition as efficient. And the snag was that he was not properly in tune with reality. That is a not very satisfactory way of putting it, but it is more accurate than saying, as many did, that he was mad, for in many ways he was piercingly sane. Perhaps the trouble was that he failed to take into account the lack of other people's sanity, to allow for the prejudices, fears, taboos and hypocrisies without which they could not function, the habitual insincerity that lubricated the mechanism of expediency.

For example, he quickly decided that most of the syllabus and all of the recommended teaching methods were irrelevant to the needs of his pupils and, before the end of the first week, scandalized parents were telephoning, writing letters or visiting the school to protest that he had been polluting the innocent minds of their off-spring by describing in detail the processes of human procreation and birth. One indignant mother of a junior girl complained that her Linda had come home and said that Mr Burberry had told her that she had once been a little fish in mummy's tummy, and an equally outraged father of one of the older boys wanted to know what kind of schoolmaster thought that a thorough knowledge of African fertility rites would help a boy to pass G.C.E. Geography. Burberry was puzzled by the complaints and even more puzzled when neither the Headmaster nor the protesting parents showed the least interest in his theories of education. He had to go, for he was regarded as a much more dangerous influence than the sub-literate Irish alcoholic who took his place, the sadistic knicker fetishist who had been there for years and the rest of the queer and crooked misfits who came and went.

The surprising thing was that one or two good teachers did stay long enough to achieve something in the way of awakening a few of the children to the excitement and nourishment that their subjects could offer. A plump, middle-aged French lady, who was not quali-fied to teach in an English state school and who was less motivated by the need for money than the wish to exercise her teaching skills, amazed us all by her firm discipline and the way she got even the most doltish and rebellious of the boys and sloppiest and idlest of the girls to work quite hard at learning her native language. But by far the best teacher in the place was James, a tough, intelligent ex-regular soldier who taught mathematics in a way that seemed to capture the enthusiasm and imagination of almost every one of his pupils. He loved his subject and he could communicate that love, originally and unpedantically. He was patient and never patronizing and he did not assume that schoolmaster's garb of omniscience which intimidates and repels. For him, teaching meant sharing in the mystery, the beauty and excitement of discovery, and, despite his passion for his subject, he was not obsessed by it. He was responsive to painting, music and literature and he was also a man of action, a good cricketer and soccer player, and he had fought a tough war in the Middle East and in Europe with the Airborne troops. And the snag here? Well, yes, there was one, but it was something that could be circumvented given a measure of tolerance which, in fact, he did receive from the Headmaster who was sensible enough to realize that he had, in James, a valuable property that was not to be lightly discarded. James's flaw was his habit of going off on periodical alcoholic jags of epic scale, on many of which I was a pie-eyed partner.

I have never, before or since, known such a drinker. At the end of the first summer term we were paid for the coming six weeks holiday. We each had about thirty pounds which, to us, was a great deal of money in those days. In less than a week we were both completely broke. I felt very close to death but James would have been only too happy to have continued his non-stop drinking for a good deal longer. His physical constitution must have been phenomenally powerful for he could swallow literally gallons of the most indigestible booze—a mixture of rough cider and Guinness was for a time a favourite potion, usually followed by bottles of the cheapest British 'port style' wine—and, although he would get very drunk, he was always ready to carry on with undiminished gusto after only four or five hours' sleep.

He was one of the few people I have known who was really funny when drunk though I admit that, since I was usually in the same state, my judgement might not be too reliable. Still, I can remember occasions which, even in retrospect, strike me as being quite comical. I had been reading Ford Madox Ford with enormous pleasure and admiration, being bowled over by *The Good Soldier* and the first three novels in the Tietjens tetralogy, *Some Do Not*, *No More Parades*, and *A Man Could Stand Up*, and I handed on to James both the books and my enthusiasm for them. We had ended up a long drinking session in a pub in Paddington one night and James, who had started that morning at 5.30 in Covent Garden, suddenly fell flat on his back. I looked down at him to see that he was still perfectly conscious and, as he gazed up at me, a huge smile spread over his face and he said slowly and distinctly, 'A man *could* stand up.'

On another night we were both arrested in Drayton Gardens for being drunk and disorderly and at the police station the solemn desk sergeant took down our particulars before we were carted off to the cells.

'Name?'

'Frederick Rolfe,' James said.

'Occupation?'

'Chemist.'

The trained ear of the sergeant must have detected a lack of veracity in James's voice. He looked more closely at his prisoner. 'What kind of chemist?'

'An alchemist,' James replied.

Soon after James came to teach at the school I left Notting Hill Gate, partly because I could not afford the fares for the daily journey and partly because I liked the district where I was working and thought that I would be able to find cheaper accommodation there. I was able to rent a quite comfortable bed-sitting room for thirty-five shillings a week and there I began to write a novel. I thought I would try something that had never been done successfully by an Englishman and only once on a small scale by an American, Ernest Hemingway, in his short story, *Fifty Grand*: that was to write a work of fiction with a background of professional boxing. I knew enough about the technicalities of the game and I understood the language fighters used and I believed that the central situation of a big title fight could serve as a useful allegory for the conflicts that seemed to underlie most personal relationships, desires and endeavours. I started to work with real excitement, writing quickly in exercise books stolen from the school stationery cupboard.

One of the difficulties that I had to try to overcome was the lack of a prepared tone and style. I had not properly realized the vast differences between the English and American languages, that the latter is peculiarly suitable for handling scenes of violence because it is itself more violent and muscular than twentieth-century indigenous English and is able naturally to *embody* violence. Proof of this can be found in the immediacy and impact of even run-of-the-mill crime fiction. Put almost any English thriller of our times against a similar American work and you will see at once that one is stiff, uneasy, clumsily theatrical, while the other is fast, supple, gritty and, within the conventions, realistic. The suitability of the American language for the depicting of vigorous action comes from the vigour of its demotic speech compared with which most of our native idiomatic language is pretty flaccid or, in the case of upper class educated speech, too bland and nicely modulated, serviceable enough for mild social satire, reflection and commentary, the evocation of moods, charting the spirit's weather, but impotent before the task of conveying the sweaty, brutal urgency of rough physical action. Contrast the American with the English popular vocabulary of abuse and invective and you will see the difference. The English, except when it is using imported idioms, is relatively mild and it lacks the Elizabethan energy, invention, gusto and savagery of the American.

I became more and more aware of the difficulty of finding a convincing and natural style as I wrote on but, of course, I did not solve the problem. I knew that imitation was not the answer but I could not see how to inject enough fire and vigour into the vocabulary, rhythms and syntax of the language that I naturally spoke and wrote. My writing slowed down, enthusiasm waned, but I carried on until I had written over two-thirds of the book and then I read it through and flung it away in disgust. It was awkward, muscle-bound, over-written and posturing. To hell with it. I stuck the exercise books away in a drawer and tried to forget about them.

I was very depressed for a time. I was twenty-nine years old, at an age when many writers had already produced fine work and, in some obvious cases, their entire and marvellous output. And I had scarcely begun, nor had I any confidence that I would ever do more than sniff around the edges of real literary creativity. In common, I imagine, with many of my generation and class, I felt a panicky sense of having left things too late, of having too much ground to make up after the shaky beginnings of an education that left you barely literate and those five years, that should have been a time of discovery and development, wasted in the khaki limbo of the infantry.

My work at the school was not much help. I found the syllabus unimaginative, the text-books were cheap, antiquated and dull and I sympathized with the class's lack of enthusiasm over their exercises in précis, comprehension and clause analysis. The children were a mixed lot. Some of the boys were obviously waiting to get out of the dump and earn some money, more or less impatient with my attempts to get them interested in anything that seemed even remotely associated with education. A few were aggressively resentful of being made to mess around with childish things while their luckier mates, who had left school at fifteen, were doing a man's job, pulling in a man's wages and enjoying a man's freedom and pleasures. One or two of the girls were equally rebellious and hostile and they were more difficult to control than the boys who, if the worst happened, could always be contained by threats of physical force; but in the main they were nice enough kids and a few showed a positive interest in and aptitude for the less stuffy work they did in English and history.

I found that I was quite good at teaching, though nothing like the dedicated natural teacher that James was. One of my successes was a boy of fourteen or so called Henry Brown. When I started at the school I was told by my predecessor and by the Headmaster that Henry was a hopeless case, scarcely literate or ever likely to be. After I had been teaching a few days he produced his essay for marking. It was an extraordinary piece of work. The handwriting was weird and rather splendid, looking from a distance like Gothic script and, at close quarters, almost impossible to read. The fact that he had virtually no idea how to spell did not help. Yet, after long and patient study of the essay I found that a kind of originality, even shafts of fitful brilliance, filtered through, even if only to be found in an occasional phrase, an odd juxtaposition of words or sudden, startlingly apt use of an epithet.

Henry was suspicious of my motives when I praised his essay.

He looked at me almost pityingly once I had convinced him that I was serious and said, as if producing incontrovertible evidence of my misjudgement, 'I'm no good at English. I'm bottom of the form.'

'Not now, you're not,' I told him, and we started to go through his essay together, word by word, his scepticism and suspicion quickly melting as his interest was engaged.

It took time, of course, but not long enough for me to grow discouraged, and once he had conceded that to spell correctly was the least you owed to the words that were serving you so well, the improvement in communicability was rapid. I had not been mistaken in seeing those gleams of originality in that first essay. He became almost fanatically absorbed in literature and the speed of his reading and the depth of his understanding were almost frightening. By the time he was fifteen he was reading things I had not got around to until I was in my twenties and, if I had not been so thrilled by his progress, I am sure I would have been jealous. He read Auden, Eliot, both the poetry and criticism, and Dylan Thomas; he actually waded through *The Interpretation of Dreams* and the shortened *Golden Bough*. He read George Eliot and Emily Brontë, Melville and Faulkner. He began to write strange and impressive little poems which suggested that he had been reading T. E. Hulme when, in fact, he had not heard of him. His critical essays on Browning and Tennyson—the set poets for his examination—were packed with independent and sometimes illuminating observations.

After he had taken his G.C.E., with exceptionally high marks in English and history and respectable results in French and Scripture, I tried to arrange for him to stay on at school to try to get a university place, but his father was not in favour of the idea and he left to take a job in a library. A few months later he wrote to me suggesting that we began '. . . a kind of Bridges–Hopkins correspondence', and there was no doubt in my mind which role he had cast me for. Improbably enough, I was to be the worthy scholarly professor who, despite his sympathy and learning, was not equipped to appreciate fully the original fire and genius of the great poet. We did write each other a few letters and he sent me five or six poems, but the inter-change became less frequent until the correspondence petered out and I have never heard of him since.

But, apart from Henry and one or two other bright and friendly youngsters, the job was monotonous and tiring, and lack of money was a constant irritation. James and I would disappear every so often during term time for two or three days' manic boozing, returning hung-over and with excuses of sore throats or touches of 'flu that we did not even bother to present convincingly and which the Headmaster preferred not to question since, apart from the French lady, we were the only two on his staff who managed to get anyone through examinations. I continued to write poems and even publish a few but I was growing more and more dissatisfied with myself and my circumstances. Then I met Elspeth.

She was a year or two older than I and she had just ended an unsatisfactory and childless marriage which had dragged on for about nine colourless years. There was something about her that attracted me strongly, a recklessness, an unaffected indifference to convention that is unusual among women and particularly women of her repressive, bottom of the scale lower-middle-class background. Her father had died when she was a little girl; her younger brother had been put into an orphanage but she had been kept at home, mainly to help her mother with the housework. She told me about her childhood without self-pity. A casual phrase in conversation or an idle anecdote from someone else might flip the switch of memory and with a kind of wondering surprise, as if the events she was de-scribing had not happened to her but to someone she had heard about, she would recall the meanness, the puritanical hatred of pleasure, the tight-lipped and hypocritical prurience, the physical and mental cruelty that her mother subjected her to, sometimes through stupidity and lack of imagination but as often from malice and resentment at being encumbered with the child of the man whom she had always despised and who had, she felt, selfishly deserted her, albeit into the forgetful kingdom of death.

Although Elspeth had missed a lot of primary education through being in hospital for many months with an attack of osteomyelitis she nevertheless won a scholarship to a girls' High School but her mother insisted on her leaving as soon as she was legally old enough. She was put to work in an estate agent's office and sent to classes in the evenings to learn shorthand and typing, which she mastered so efficiently that she was able later to get the post, which she held when I first met her, teaching these skills in a private college of commerce.

We had known each other for only a few days when we decided to look for somewhere to live together and we found a two-roomed flat at a very moderate rent and set up home. Soon after we had moved in I was sorting out my papers and books when I came across the manuscript of the almost finished novel that I had started the previous year and, before throwing it into the dustbin, I began to glance through it. After skimming a few pages I turned back to the beginning and started to read it carefully, finding it not so bad as I had believed, even coming across passages that were quite gripping. So I decided to finish it. With Elspeth to provide for my material needs, to cook, launder and supply restorative coffee, I was able to work steadily in the evenings and at weekends and during the Easter break of 1952 I finished it.

Elspeth said, 'Let me have it. I'll type it for you.'

'You wouldn't be able to read my writing.'

She looked at the scribbled pages, some of which I had great difficulty myself in deciphering, and she had to admit I was right.

Then she said, 'It doesn't matter. You read it to me. I'll take it down in shorthand and then I can type it.'

And that is what we did. In less than two weeks she presented me with a faultlessly typed script and carbon copy of the book to which I had given the title, *The Fight*.

I hope to God that I showed enough appreciation though I fear that I did not. Elspeth's devotion, her belief, however misplaced, in my talent as a writer, her generosity and passion still reproach me. I was not worthy of them, nor of her. This must sound like those maudlin confessions of old rakes who are really boasting, whose self-flagellations are so gentle that they are masturbatory, but the truth is that I am still nagged by the memory of my complacent acceptance of all that she gave, of my laziness and lack of consideration. And yet she must have got something out of the relationship, apart, that is, from the sexual fulfilment that we both enjoyed. Her husband had been a man with absolutely no interests outside his job as a civil servant and his enormous collection of foreign stamps. He never read a book, watched a film or listened to music. At least I was able to encourage and even guide her reading which she had neglected since girlhood and was now rediscovering with delight. Like many self-taught people I got special pleasure from imparting to others what I had learnt, and Elspeth was an eager and touchingly grateful pupil. Not that she was intellectually servile: she would argue her point of view, even to the extent of exasperating me so much that I would lose patience and start bombarding her with invective which she would do her best to throw back; we often finished up flushed and angry until we saw how absurd we were being, then laughter would be followed by apologies and reassurances that led to strenuous reconciliation in bed.

She was very excited about the novel. 'Where are you going to send it?' she said. 'I bet any publisher would snap it up.'

I was less confident but since the thing was completed and so beautifully typed I knew I would offer it to some publisher. A little while previously I had met Margaret Crosland, a poet and French translator who was married to a literary agent and acted as his assistant since they had no children at that time. I gave her *The Fight* to read and she was very enthusiastic about it and suggested that I let her husband act as my agent. I agreed, and a few weeks later she told me that they had offered the novel to a small but ambitious publisher called Peter Nevill who was very keen to take the book on. I could hardly believe my luck until the contracts were signed and I was paid the first half of my advance, twenty-five pounds.

The pathetic smallness of the sum did not depress me or Elspeth. What did it matter, she argued. Once the book was published it would get marvellous reviews, sell in thousands, and I would collect large sums in royalties. Again, I was less confident than she, but I was encouraged to start work on another novel.

I was back at the school and finding the job more tedious than ever. Every couple of weeks or so I would launch myself on a heavy drinking session, often in the company of James, and on these occasions some small disaster usually befell us. We were quite often arrested and had to spend a night in the cells, and one night I got back to the flat with my head cut open and my shirt and coat soaked in blood. Poor Elspeth had to telephone for an ambulance and I was carted round to the hospital to have eight stitches put into the back of my damaged cranium. I could not remember how I had sustained the injury. Yet I managed to keep working pretty hard. Apart from the novel, I was writing poems and I tried some short stories which were not much good but more likely to earn some money than the poems. In fact two of them did: they were broadcast on the radio Morning Story and I think I was paid ten guineas for each. Then I had a letter from a BBC producer called Paul Stephenson. He had met somebody who had known me in my boxing days and he was intrigued by what he regarded as the piquant mixture of poetry and pugilism. Would I be interested in giving a radio talk, perhaps explaining the attraction for me of these two contrasted activities, or on another subject that we could together agree on? He suggested that I should ring him up and we could meet for a drink and a chat.

As a result of our meeting I wrote a script about fairground boxing booths and I delivered it, live, at a peak listening hour some time in the middle of the evening. Television had not yet taken over from radio, and criticism of sound programmes was given a good deal of space in the newspapers; regular broadcasters, whatever their speciality—and indeed some of the most successful seemed to have no speciality—rapidly became famous and, presumably, rich. My own talk was reviewed by quite a few newspapers and I remember Maurice Wiggin writing quite warmly about it in the *Sunday Times*. The script had taken me only three evenings to write and I had been paid fifteen guineas for it. Paul Stephenson seemed quite anxious that I should do more talks. Suddenly it appeared that an escape route had been opened for me to get out of the teaching job into the more spacious and rewarding field of free-lance broadcasting, and not only would I be financially better off but I would have far more time for serious writing. Elspeth was just as excited by the prospect as I was, so I handed in my notice and left my job at the end of the summer term.

*

At first things were not too bad. I did more radio talks but these were broadcast on a morning programme which attracted fewer listeners and gained little or no kudos, and though I continued to sell a few poems to the weeklies these were poorly paid. I found that I was depending largely on Elspeth's earnings while I worked without much real involvement and far too quickly and carelessly on the novel. It was not long before tension developed between Elspeth and me. For some time she had been feeling dissatisfied with her job, convinced that her abilities, real and potential, were being given no chance to expand, and she began to look out for a way of escape into wider and richer fields. I was in entire sympathy with her and when she saw an advertisement offering places at a Teachers' Training College for 'mature students' who were experienced in commerce or industry, we both decided that it would be a good idea for her to apply for entry.

I think we knew that this would lead to the dissolution of our relationship. The college was residential and, while she would receive a financial grant, it would be barely sufficient for her own needs. If she were to leave the flat I certainly could not on my own afford to pay the rent. She was determined to break away from her frustrating job but she was worried about what would happen to me when I was left on my own, and her anxiety created further tensions, because I regarded it as a criticism of my capacity for looking after myself and I think she resented me, though probably unconsciously, as the origin and aggravation of her predicament. But our failure to remain together had deeper causes than these, for the truth was that I had never been able to give her the totally committed love she hungered for and deserved.

I was then thirty years old and I had been through a number of affairs, but had known that each one was temporary, that the girl was not the one I was prepared to spend the rest of my days with, so that I was never completely absorbed in the shared life. I was—though not always consciously—rather like the man who dances smoothly and enjoyably enough with the woman in his arms but keeps flicking a glance round the floor for another and more attractive partner. I do not think I was especially sentimental in my view of romantic love, believing in the existence of an ideal, predestined

Miss Right, yet I was sure it would be a mistake to marry unless the decision involved the consent of the whole being, allowing for not the least thread of doubt or reservation. The example of my own parents, of my brother and the many friends who had married for reasons that were not inevitable and irreversible counselled wariness. I did not believe that I would necessarily meet anyone who would arouse in me such a totality of desire, and the possibility that, if I did, my feelings would not be mirrored in her own seemed more than likely; but even if it meant an old age of loneliness and frustration, shabby and obscene counterfeits for human warmth, I was resolved not to be sidetracked into one of those grey nuptial dungeons where I would be held prisoner by habit, weariness and the insidious agoraphobia of an interminable sentence.

Elspeth was given a place at the training college where she was to take up residence in October. I had only a few weeks in which to find new lodgings. By working for over ten hours a day I managed to finish the novel at a breathless gallop and get it accepted by the same publisher for the same advance of fifty pounds in two parts. As soon as the cheque for twenty-five pounds arrived I sought out James, who was still teaching at the school, and invited him to join me in a celebratory drink.

James had never much cared for Elspeth, regarding her as an over-earnest blue-stocking and a not very well filled one at that, and he welcomed the news that she and I were parting. We were drinking in a little pub that was used mainly by tough old ladies with cherries on their hats, market-traders and horsey men in check caps who spat.

James said, 'You're well out of it. She'd have had your balls off. You'll be able to get some real work done now.'

'Maybe. But I've got to find somewhere to live first.'

'Don't worry. I know the very place. It'll be dead cheap. An old friend of mine lives not more than a mile from here. Pike is his name. He calls himself a psychologist. He's a bit weird but worth seeing as a biological specimen. I used to stay with him myself. Come on, let's go and look him up. We'd better take a couple of bottles.'

We caught a bus to the rather dismal suburb where in a street of solid, identical houses Pike practised his strange arts and lived his strange life. His wife, Lil, opened the door to us. She was a big woman of about thirty with untidy hair and dazed eyes, sloppily dressed with the sort of carelessness that can be disturbingly suggestive of other kinds of carelessness, of undone buttons and zips and left-off underwear and of a moral negligence that often goes with the physical.

Light momentarily flickered in her eyes when she saw the bottles we were carrying.

'Lovely to see you, James,' she said. 'Come on in.' She smiled at me. 'You a drunken pisspot like James?' she enquired amiably.

James introduced me and we went into the kitchen at the back of the house where I met Pike who was sitting at the table reading an evening paper. He wore a coat that had once been white and was now very grimy, and from what could be seen of his shirt it looked as if it had been worn day and night for a fortnight. His hair was coarse and fair and it grew low on his narrow forehead. One eye squinted in towards his thin, suspicious nose and his upper lip was stained a curious orange colour, presumably from the cigarettes of which he seemed always to have an inexhaustible supply and which he smoked between his lips, never taking them out of his mouth until they were reduced to little more than glowing embers and letting the ash grow until it drooped and fell, powdering his front with its grey fall-out.

The four of us sat at the table and drank wine. It was arranged that I would move in at the beginning of the following week and that I would pay five pounds a month for my room. If I wished to eat any of my meals with them, we could agree on reasonable extra charges. Lil showed me the room I was to occupy. It was very small and narrow, not really a bedroom at all, and it contained nothing but a chair and camp-bed with what looked like army blankets on it. I was not much taken with either the room or the Pikes but I thought I could not afford to turn down such cheap accommodation.

As I got to know them better they began to exercise over me a certain hideous fascination. They were so utterly depraved. I could have imagined them more happily occupied in an earlier century that would have allowed their special kind of craven avarice and ruthlessness greater scope, as for instance a murderous nurse and watchman in the Great Plague. James had warned me of their eccentricity and of their nastiness, which he found—or pretended to find—more intriguing than I did, and he solemnly maintained that to know the Pikes was to add a new dimension to the concept of the human. I soon began to understand what he meant.

I learnt that I could not leave anything of the slightest value lying around, especially money, for one or other of my hosts would steal it without hesitation and without shame. When I did complain, first about a pair of shoes that Pike had hocked and afterwards about a missing five shillings, they said I should be more careful with my possessions.

'Anyway,' Pike said, 'you've got a good pair of shoes on. You can't wear two pairs at once.'

Their sex-life was pretty shameless, too. I would have preferred to remain in ignorance but this was difficult since they obviously enjoyed the stimulus of an audience. One evening, four or five days after I had moved in and when we had just returned from the local pub where the drinks had been provided by me, with never an offer from Pike, we were sitting in the kitchen and Pike suddenly heaved Lil on to the table and began to ride her, yipping and whooping like a rodeo star. I hurried out and went up to my room, but the noises of their violent coupling pursued me, going on for an extraordinarily long time with an effect that, far from being titillating, would be more likely to put you off sex for life.

My hasty departure from the exhibition afforded them a lot of amusement and they obviously thought I was a prissy fellow with the susceptibilities of a Victorian curate. Lil usually treated me with a friendly, half-contemptuous motherliness, though once or twice, probably through sheer habit, she would become flirtatious and then I noticed a dangerous glitter in Pike's squinting eyes. I am sure that for him jealousy worked aphrodisiacally but it also awakened a menacing hostility and I guessed that he was quite capable of putting a knife in your back. James told me that, in the days when he was living there, Pike had more than once sent Lil out on to the streets to earn a few pounds and when she had returned he had taken whatever money she had been able to make, beaten her up for her infidelity and then fucked her in a lather of vengeful passion.

You might well wonder why I stayed with the Pikes. As I said, I must admit that there was something fascinating about them. Pike, as might be expected, was totally incompetent as a psychologist but, despite this fact and his well-deserved reputation for drunkenness and lechery, a few patients still came to him for treatment. One afternoon I happened to be going into the house at the same time as one such patient, a middle-aged, haunted-looking man who certainly looked in need of treatment. Lil showed the man into what they grandly called the consulting room and, as I went upstairs, I heard her calling her husband. About ten minutes later, Pike came up to my room and said, 'Did you see that chap I've just been treating? He's just shot out of here like a frightened rabbit. Sod it. I thought I'd got twenty sessions there but the bugger must think he's cured already!'

No woman under the age of sixty came for treatment more than once and, by the time I became part of the household, Pike's practice did not supply them with anything like enough money to live on. He was prepared to do anything—except honest work—to make a few pounds. When he took a job as temporary postman at Christmas he examined his sacks of mail for anything that was of value and destroyed the stuff that was of no interest. He owned collecting-boxes for various charities and quite often, on a Friday or Saturday night, he and Lil would take a bus to a district where they were not known and go round the pubs collecting for spastics or the blind.

Another bright idea of Pike's was for Lil to make meat pies which they would supply to local publicans and to the owner of the coffee stall on the main street. They got hold of some cheap horse-meat and Lil, who was quite a resourceful woman at the stove when she could bother to be, worked hard through the morning, cooking about five dozen pies which Pike peddled during the lunchtime session, having a couple of drinks in each of the pubs he visited. By closing-time he had sold the pies but, after all the drinks he had enjoyed at the various bars and after stocking up with cigarettes and a couple of bottles to sustain him through the afternoon, he had spent all the money. So he ordered Lil to cook more pies which he would be able to sell in the evening.

She said that she could not make more because all the meat had been used up.

'Bugger the meat,' Pike said. 'You can stick something in them, can't you? In any case, if you don't put any filling in at all, nobody's going to be any the wiser till after I've got the money and cleared off. That's it. Just do the crusts and stick a bit of old bread or something inside to give a bit of weight. I'll get a bus to the Green and flog 'em there. I'll have disappeared by the time anybody finds out what they've got inside.'

So Pike sold his bread pies to the unsuspecting publicans in an area where he hoped no one would know him and he and Lil spent the proceeds on a wild evening's drinking.

Part of the reluctant and horrified fascination that Pike awakened in me was similar to the uneasy feelings of attraction and revulsion that freaks and monsters evoke, and also because he and his wife seemed more like grotesque characters in fiction than most of the people one meets in quotidian life. But it was not long before I had had enough, though I was held there by poverty.

Early in 1953 *The Fight* was published, but I had already borrowed most of the second part of the advance from my agent. The novel was, on the whole, quite favourably received and, for a first book by an almost unknown writer, it sold quite well, going through the first printing of three thousand copies and a second impression of a thousand, but I never seemed to have enough money in hand to move from the Pikes. Then I had a stroke of luck. The BBC Third Programme had just introduced a new series called, if I remember correctly, *First Hearing*, each broadcast being an anthology of new poetry and prose, something like a *Penguin New Writing* of the air. John Wain, who selected and introduced one of these programmes, used some of my poems for which I was paid quite well, enough at any rate for me to be able to escape from the Pikes and move into a relatively comfortable room in a house near the Common. The rent was fifty shillings a week and I knew that I would not be able to keep up the payments unless I found a more regular source of income.

Again I was lucky. I met a young playwright named John Hall who was working for a recently established crammer's not far from where I was living, and he introduced me to the Principal, giving me a big build-up as a published poet and novelist and skating cagily round the matter of academic qualifications. The result was that I was taken on to coach English and history for five hours each working day, for which I was to be paid ten shillings an hour, or twelve pounds ten a week. This sum seemed princely to me and I settled down to a more productive and contented life. I was again able to read and write for my own satisfaction rather than for the sole purpose of making enough money to keep alive on, and I was happier than I had been for some time. I still saw James at intervals and often drank too much, but I managed to keep working steadily both at my writing and teaching.

In the summer—it must have been June or early July—I received a letter from my old friend, Kenneth Severs, who had given up his lectureship at Hatfield College and joined the BBC Northern Region as a Talks Producer. He wrote that he was coming to London for a couple of days and he suggested that we should meet outside Broadcasting House at noon on the coming Saturday. He would be returning to Leeds the following morning but at least we could have a lovely day together. I remember that meeting very clearly.

It was one of those sparkling days when the act of breathing is a conscious pleasure, when not even the faintest smudge of darkness has been left on the fair body of the morning, when you know that nothing can happen that will not be welcome and, as you walk along the road, you find yourself moving to a silent music. I had money in my pocket, I felt strong and buoyantly healthy, the sun glittered on the traffic at Oxford Circus and, as I walked towards Broadcasting House, I saw the inviting day stretched before me like an unwritten poem. I arrived a few minutes early for the meeting and I stood on the pavement watching the tourists in their large, alien hats with cameras slung about their necks like amulets, the bare arms and legs of girls in flowery dresses, their hair gleaming in sunlight—all the dear clichés of summer in the city. I felt both excited yet contented, quite happy to wait without impatience, enjoying the warmth and colour and movement about me. Then I heard my name being called.

An old red sports car had pulled up at the kerb and there was Kenneth Severs, waving from the passenger seat, and at the wheel was a dark, smiling girl.

He said, 'Come on. Hop in the back.'

I climbed in and we drove around until we found a space where we could park the car and then we went into The George and ordered beers, drinking them at the bar.

The girl's name was Jo and she taught painting at the Leeds College of Art. Her home was in Kent and she had given Kenneth a lift down since she intended visiting her parents for the weekend before travelling to Italy for a few months as a consequence of winning the Rome Prize for painting. She seemed rather shy, but not gauche, happier to listen to us talking about our concerns than to discuss her own, and willing to go along with whatever we wanted to do. Not that she was negative or over-anxious to please. You sensed her intelligence and humour and she impressed by not making the least attempt to impress. I liked her very much and thought she had unusually beautiful eyes.

After the pub shut we drove off in Jo's car to visit Kenneth's married brother who lived somewhere in the Earls Court district, and in the evening we went to a party at the BBC Club given by a London friend and colleague of Kenneth's who was giving up his staff job to free-lance as a radio broadcaster. I got Jo to myself for quite a long time at the party, when Kenneth must have been involved elsewhere with business talk, and I remember becoming more attracted to her and growing steadily more envious of Kenneth whom I took to be either her prospective or actual lover. I expect I showed off. I certainly drank a great deal and before the party came to an end I was almost out on my feet. I have no recollection of saying goodbye to Jo or Kenneth or my host but I do vaguely remember lurching towards a tilted Oxford Circus Underground Station to catch a train back to Ealing, drunken sleep and the long, eclipsing hangover of a lonely Sunday. When I was sufficiently recovered the next day to think constructively about the previous day's events, I thought I could remember writing down Jo's surname and address, but after repeated searchings of all my pockets I had to give up. Although I might never see her again I knew that I would not easily forget her.

*

The summer softened into autumn and my life continued to be on the whole pleasant and satisfying. I wrote a lot of verse but destroyed much of it, having enough sense to realize that I was shadow-boxing, getting the muscles limber for the real encounters, if ever they should occur. Then, without warning, my peaceful existence was threatened. At the beginning of October, the Principal called his staff together for a meeting and announced that the business had been losing too much money and, unless he cut down on expenses, he would be bankrupt within two or three months. Regretfully he would have to terminate the employment of the more recent additions to the teaching staff and ask those who remained to take on extra teaching duties without extra remuneration. I knew that, as the last to join, I would be the first to go. It was agreed that I should stay until the end of the month so, at the beginning of November, I found myself once again without regular employment.

I had managed to save a little money and the publication of my second novel brought me in another twenty-five pounds, so I was not concerned for the time being about getting another job. Foolishly I celebrated the birth of my second novel with a party which began in a pub with James and a couple of other drinking friends and ended in my room with at least a dozen people squeezed into it, including some shrill women whose midnight voices brought my landlady hurrying to investigate. She was so shocked by the scenes of licence that she told me I would have to leave the premises the very next morning. There might have been a faint chance of talking her round if we had not been so drunk but the poor woman was driven away by wild laughter, derisive gestures and coarse remarks.

The following day I packed my possessions and moved to the Pikes, resolved not to stay there for more than a few days. I was lucky enough to be able to escape within the week. Some friends of mine, Peter and Margaret Tillott who were living then in West-bourne Grove, knew of a flat that had just become vacant in Craven Terrace in Paddington. It had been occupied by an historian colleague of Peter's, a gentle scholarly man who had contracted tuberculosis and would be away for an unspecified but obviously quite lengthy period and who wished to sub-let at no more than the rent he himself paid—which was very modest since he had first taken the place, unfurnished, in the days of the Blitz and his frustrated landlord was powerless to increase the monthly sum. Of course, I jumped at the chance and I moved in on a wet November afternoon when the street lamps and shop windows were lighting up prematurely against the shroud of mist and rain. And that is how I remember Craven Terrace: furred lamps in the mist, the seal-back surface of the road, a few mushed leaves in the gutters, a little backwater where it was always late autumn.

The flat was large but very draughty and damp and I was not surprised that its former tenant had fallen sick, but its look of shabby splendour pleased me and it was a joy, after living for so long in cramped conditions, to have plenty of space. There was a large living-room with loaded bookshelves on three of the walls, a fair-sized bedroom, a kitchen and bathroom. The books were mainly devoted to medieval history though there were a few old-fashioned popular novels by authors like Rider Haggard, Bulwer Lytton and Harrison Ainsworth and a number of Oxford editions of the poets, a forbidding Spenser with minute type and two columns to each page, a much more inviting Milton and the Bohn's Standard Library edition of Cary's Dante. There was also a good deal of heavyweight theology and some useful books of reference. You could smell the mould of the damp pages everywhere, at first rather sickening but soon to become simply the smell of home.

I was already becoming short of money after having paid a month's rent in advance and I knew that I had to get down to some hack work straight away. I wrote a couple of pieces for *Everybody's Weekly*, one for the literary editor, Kenneth Hopkins, on Alun Lewis, and the other for the sports editor, Colonel Dudley Lister, former A.B.A. Heavyweight Champion, on the contemporary state of professional boxing; and for each of these I was paid fifteen guineas. Ludovic Kennedy had taken over the Third Programme *First Hearing* from John Wain and he used three of my poems which were again well paid. Kennedy also introduced a literary competition inviting listeners to submit a parody of Graham Greene's prose, so I entered for this, using my old ring name of John Bain. I received another ten guineas when my piece was judged to have won. These were my most remunerative activities.

Less well paid, or not paid at all, were the poems in magazines and the two short scripts I wrote for BBC Overseas Service.

The annual P.E.N. anthologies, *New Poems*, had just started and two things of mine were printed in the 1953 volume. A rather splendid party was given for the contributors at the P.E.N. centre in Glebe Place, Chelsea, where the older and better fed guests must have been disconcerted, if not appalled, by the rapid decline into staggering drunkenness among the mainly younger and underfed poets, knocked silly by the unaccustomed short and powerful drinks. For me events soon became blurred and, when I woke up the next morning and padded muzzily from bedroom into living-room, I was surprised to find the long and bony form of the poet, John Heath-Stubbs, spread out on the couch covered by rugs and coats. I made tea and woke him and, while we sipped and smoked, he told me that he had been concerned for my safety on the previous night and had decided to accompany me home. Even then, John's eye-sight was very weak and, though his hangover was not as crushing as mine, I am sure he had not gone without drink himself, so it is doubtful that his presence had much reduced the perils of the journey, but I was grateful for his good intentions.

At that party I met for the first time many people whom I was later to know better: Roy Fuller, looking young enough to be his own son, Laurie Lee who seems scarcely to have changed in almost two decades, and Robert Conquest, on the surface very public school, Oxford and Foreign Office, showing little or nothing of the tough-minded, witty and original character I was later to admire. Stevie Smith was there, black-haired then, just as elfin, with eyes like amused and very clever currants, Dannie Abse, Thomas Blackburn and Michael Hamburger who were to become good friends.

The Christmas of 1953 was a bleak occasion for me. Most of my single friends were out of London and I did not feel like intruding on the married ones, so I stayed on my own and felt sorry for myself. The weather at the beginning of the new year was unusually mild and, when I was not working or reading, I walked, covering miles of London streets and getting to know intimately many previously unfamiliar districts. Money was now very short. I wrote and delivered another radio talk, produced this time by Richard Keen, and I sold poems to the newly established *London Magazine* and *Encounter*, but I still had to borrow from my agent and I knew that there would be little or nothing in royalties to come from the novels by the time I had paid him back.

One day, in February or early March, I was in The George with a friend who was a features producer with the BBC and in chatting over our drinks he asked me if I had listened to a commentary on the title fight which had been broadcast on the previous night. I said that I had heard it but I had been irritated by the commentator who clearly knew little about the game and spent far too much time describing the boxers' gear and physical appearance, trying to produce apt metaphors and memorable phrases when he should have been telling listeners, quickly and simply, what was going on in the ring.

My friend said, 'Why don't you apply for an audition? You've done a bit of broadcasting. You know the game. I'd have thought it'd be right up your street.'

At first I was doubtful: the job of a professional sports commentator appeared so distant from the literary role that it seemed impossible that they could ever be united. Yet, on further reflection, I began to warm to the idea. After all, I loved boxing, I knew a good bit about it and I was reasonably articulate. I would be at the ringside at every big fight and would be paid handsomely for being there. And the beauty of it was that there would be no irksome preparations for each job, no scripts to be written, no tedious rehearsals. The more I thought of it the more inviting the prospect became.

I wrote to the Head of Outside Broadcasts, setting out what I considered to be my qualifications, and a few days later I was interviewed by him and an audition was arranged. This meant that I was to go to the next boxing promotion that the BBC was covering and, after the live commentary had been broadcast, I would take over the microphone for one of the preliminary bouts and commentate for a couple of rounds. My performance, of course, would not go on the air but would be recorded at Broadcasting House for its quality to be judged later.

At the time it was the BBC's policy to broadcast commentaries from the smaller promotions and the place I was sent to was Watford Town Hall where, almost ten years earlier, I had boxed in a six-rounder. After Raymond Glendenning had commentated on the main event—in my not noticeably humble opinion, ineptly—I was installed at the ringside with the microphone. The next bout was over eight rounds between a couple of lightweights named—maliciously—Cole and Rowley who, as often as not, in my flurried account of the battle, became Roll and Cowley. When the allotted two rounds were finished I was sweating more than either of the fighters and I relinquished the microphone with relief, had a drink in the bar and returned to Craven Terrace. A few days later a letter from the BBC arrived telling me that my commentary had been assessed and found inadequate. If I wished, I could go to Broadcasting House and listen to the recording and to an official explanation of my deficiencies. I did not go.

Then I suffered a vicious attack of spring 'flu and lay in my damp bedroom, sweating and shivering and aching, too sick and miserable to do anything about getting myself well. I was in bed for five days before I got up, feeling balloon-headed and rubber-limbed, but free at last from the fever. I had no money at all.

After a bath and a shave I floated downstairs and began to drift towards Marble Arch. A strong breeze would have picked me up and whisked me over the treetops in the park. I visited the office of my agent and persuaded him, not without difficulty, to part with two pound-notes. Then I went to a cheap Italian restaurant in Greek Street and ordered minestrone and ravioli, but the soup proved almost as much as I could manage and I could not swallow more than a couple of mouthfuls of the ravioli. I drank a cup of coffee and then walked back to Craven Terrace. I tried to read but could not concentrate at all. I felt that I needed company yet could think of no one I wished to see, and I was troubled by the kind of mild, unfocused randiness that is often one of the minor symptoms of a hangover, a sexual itch that could not be scratched, that was somehow out of reach. The thought of actual fulfilment was untempting, not what I wanted at all. This was a metaphysical sexuality and it was oddly unpleasant.

I had expected to feel better the next day, but I did not, nor for the next few days. I found that I slept scarcely at all, although I tried to exhaust myself with long walks. I still found it impossible to read with any pleasure or much understanding, and writing was out of the question. I felt vaguely ill and held firmly down by the kind of creative impotence that the Americans call a 'block', so it was bad luck that I should at that time receive a letter from Stephen Spender who, with Melvin Lasky, was co-editor of *Encounter* asking me to go to the office of the magazine for a chat about doing some reviewing. It was the kind of chance I had long been waiting for and it had come at a time when I was least able to take advantage of it.

I had not met Spender before and I was surprised by his great height. From people who knew him, or professed to know him, I had heard a lot of malicious comment which I can only put down to jealousy or pure bitchiness because I found him then, as I have since on the few occasions that we have met or communicated by letter, a man of great kindness, intelligence and integrity. We talked in the shabby office above Haymarket about his recently published critical book, *The Creative Element*, about literature in general and poetry in particular. He was modest, without a trace of self-importance, and he seemed genuinely interested in anything I had to say. Before I left he apologized that he had not much of interest that he could offer me for reviewing unless I would like to do a piece on *Under Milk Wood*. Without thinking, I agreed to write something and I took the book away when I left.

It was not until I got back to the flat that I realized that I should not have taken on the job. Already, so soon after Thomas's death, far too much had been written about this particular work and about the man himself, and since I could scarcely bring myself to write a brief personal letter and was still finding it almost impossible to respond to any kind of literature, I was the least likely person to add anything of value. But I needed the money so badly that I forced myself with great difficulty to write a review, not a word of which I can recall and not one of which, I am quite sure, would be worth the effort. Heaven knows what Spender thought when the tired, muddled farrago of half-baked comment and judgement reached him, but what he did was write a sympathetic letter saying

164

that he did not think the tone of the piece quite right for *Encounter*, hinting that perhaps criticism was not my *métier*, and hoping that I would not be too put out by the rejection. Then he added: 'It is not important. You write good poetry and that is all that matters.' I cannot think of many other hard-worked editors who would have gone to the same trouble to spare the feelings and boost the confidence of a little-known writer.

I was grateful for and touched by the letter but my confidence was not buttressed. On the contrary, what little I had ever possessed seeped away completely and I was strait-jacketed by an emasculating ennui and apathy which I could not struggle out of. I would get out of bed each morning, after a virtually sleepless night, and I would drink some tea and perhaps eat a slice of toast. Then I would sit around feeling tired and incapable of even attempting to read or work. After an hour or so of this I would leave the flat and walk for as long as four or five hours and come back and sit down again, feeling just as I had before I left. I was tired of London and tired of life.

I cannot imagine what would have happened had not a letter from my brother arrived. He had gone to Dundee and was working in a bookshop which had a coffee room in the basement where customers could enjoy refreshment and conversation after they had made their purchases. The proprietor had gone abroad for a few weeks and Kenneth wondered if I could travel north and work there during the boss's absence. Suddenly I knew that this was just what I needed, a complete change of surroundings and a simple job to do. By another stroke of good fortune one of my radio talks was repeated and the *Spectator* bought two poems, so I was able to pay my rent until the end of the month and still have enough left for my fare to Dundee which would be refunded when I got there.

Travelling to Dundee was like moving on a time-machine back to the 1920s. Although it was the end of spring the city was dark and wind-worried and cold. Not far from the centre were the jute mills and the gaol-like tenement buildings where the workers lived in exactly the same conditions as their oppressed parents and grandparents had lived, with the cold water sink and the spluttering gas mantles, the outside lavatory on the 'stair' which had to serve five or six families. Kenneth lived in one of these buildings though we used his place only for sleeping in, spending the rest of our time at the bookshop or in the bars of the city where undersized, bandy-legged men in cloth caps and mufflers drank joylessly.

The stay in Dundee was good for me. I did not attempt to write anything and I read little apart from newspapers and a few novels. Kenneth and I drank a fair amount but shortage of money and the Scottish licensing hours kept our consumption down to a decent limit. I enjoyed working in the bookshop and serving coffee in the place below and was quite sorry when, after three weeks, Kenneth said that his employer was returning in a few days. But I did not go straight back to London.

On the day after my arrival in Dundee I had seen an advertisement in one of the daily papers inviting applications for a job as Programme Assistant with the BBC Northern Region in Leeds and, tempted by what was, by my standards, a huge salary and by fond memories of Leeds, I had written to offer my services. Just before I left Dundee the Leeds people wrote and invited me for an interview, so I stayed in Scotland with Kenneth until the day before my appointment and I arrived in Leeds with nearly nine pounds in my pocket and happy in the certainty of being able to claim travelling expenses from the BBC.

Kenneth Severs was on the interviewing board but I did not get the job which I believe was given to a man already working for the Corporation in London. Kenneth and I met for a drink that evening and he put me up for the night. The next day I took a tram down to Briggate and went into Whitelocks and found some of my old drinking companions, among them Bernard Brett and Ratz Scriven. It was Derby Day and there was a lot of chat in the pub about the various runners but it meant nothing to me for I have never taken the least interest in horse-racing. After an hour or so of drinking someone suggested going to the illicit betting-shop that crouched darkly in a furtive alley very close to the pub and, since everybody seemed interested, I went along too. Once in the place I decided that I might as well have a bet. The list of runners was chalked on a blackboard hanging on the wall. One horse was called Never Say Die and it was being ridden by a young jockey named Lester Piggott.

Why not? I thought. You were always hearing of beginners' luck. Maybe there was some truth in it.

I said to one of the company who knew something about gambling, 'Put a pound on Never Say Die for me, will you?'

'To win?'

The question seemed idiotic. I had never heard of anyone backing a horse to lose. 'Of course,' I said.

'Never Say Die? It's an outsider. Doesn't stand a chance.'

'I'll risk it.'

'Okay. It's your money.'

When we had placed our bets we returned to the pub and at closing time we moved off to a café where it was customary for those who had no more pressing business to while away the time over coffee until the pubs opened again for the evening session.

As the waitress was serving me, Ratz said to me, 'Did you back anything?'

My earlier optimism had gone sour. I said gloomily, 'Yes. I'm a damned fool. Don't know a thing about horses and I put a pound on an outsider.'

'What was it called?'

'Never Say Die.'

The waitress finished setting down our coffees and walked away. A few minutes later she appeared from the kitchen, looking flushed and excited, and she ran to our table.

'Didn't I hear one of you gentlemen say he'd backed Never Say Die?' she said. 'It's just won at thirty-three to one!'

I stayed one more night in Leeds but I was ready to move back to London the next day. Leeds had lost a lot of its old magic. I would always feel an affection for the place but I could not deceive myself that we could now live together for any length of time. I treated myself to a half bottle of Mâcon with my lunch on the train to King's Cross and when I got back to Craven Terrace I set to and vigorously cleaned up the flat. The crisis of health, mental or physical or both, was over. My northern trip had pulled me through and I knew that I would now be able to get down to some work.

*

I did work, very steadily, for the next few weeks and, under a pen-name, I wrote a collection of simple stories from English history for the publisher who had taken my other book for children. I sold it for an outright payment of seventy-five pounds, but I knew that the kind of life I was leading was in most ways unsatisfactory and unlikely to provide the circumstances in which I could settle down to more serious work and study.

It was late in June and the fine weather constantly tempted me out of the musty twilight of the flat and awakened yearnings, no less strong for being imprecise, for a less solitary existence. I walked in Kensington Gardens and watched the lovers strolling in the sun or lying close together on the grass and I felt more keenly than ever before that sustained ache of loneliness that is both painful yet curiously enjoyable, a sensation that can never properly be known outside a great city with its flaunting indifference, its stone-hearted glamour. Sometimes I succumbed to the temptation of ringing up one of the few available girls I knew, but when I met one I found that I was bored and irritable and, though I would glumly see the thing through, I knew that I was hungering for something more nourishing and permanent than the tired parody of seduction, the reflex acrobatics on divan or bed. When the quick lay failed to ease the loneliness and accidie the pub beckoned and I fell into the trap repeatedly, knowing that I was in danger of becoming one of those solitary, middle-aged boozers you see in every big city bar, knocking back the drinks too fast, trying not to show the effect of the alcohol and eyeing the other, the unlonely cheerful drinkers—especially the women—without hope, their eyes pleading yet aggrieved and bitter with resentment and envy.

Then, one early evening, I had wandered along to Notting Hill Gate and decided I must postpone drinking for an hour or so if I was to stay on my feet until closing-time. So I bought an evening paper and went into a coffee bar where I could sit and read in comfort. I asked for a cup of coffee at the counter, found a seat at one of the window tables and opened my newspaper. As I had ordered the coffee I had been vaguely aware of a girl sitting on one of the stools at the counter but I had not looked closely at her. When I lowered my paper to stick a cigarette in my mouth and light it I sensed that she was looking at me. I glanced up at her and recognized her instantly. It was the painter, Jo, whom I had last seen at the BBC Club party with Kenneth Severs.

I left the table and went across to her. 'Aren't you—'

She broke in: 'Yes, I thought I recognized you when you came in. How nice to see you.'

She joined me at my table and I told her something of what I had been doing since we had last met and she told me a little about her stay in Italy.

I said, 'And when do you go back to Leeds?'

'I'm not going back.'

I was surprised. 'Have you given up the job?'

'Yes. I gave it up when I went abroad.'

'Where are you living?'

'Here, in London. Just round the corner, Kensington Park Gardens.'

My heart did a quick somersault. I tried to caution myself, not show my pleasure, but I knew I must have looked delighted.

I tried to sound casual, 'Are you busy? I mean if you're not doing anything special, we could go and have a drink.'

'A good idea,' she said at once.

We went to a pub called The Chepstow and we stayed there until the place closed, by which time I had discovered that I had been mistaken in believing that there was any serious relationship between her and Kenneth Severs, that she was not at that moment committed to any one man and that she was the woman I wanted to marry. I could see the possibility of escaping from the loneliness, frustration and drabness that had been threatening to claim me for good. I felt her sympathy and warmth and the light touch of intelligence and I saw, once or twice, the flicker of humour and the strength of a robust scepticism. I cannot say she was the kind of woman I liked, for I had met no other woman quite like her. She was herself, unique, inimitable and already so precious to me that I was in a fever of apprehension in case I should lose her; and yet, beneath that fear, I believe that there was a strong undercurrent of certainty and I think she felt the same.

We saw each other every spare moment for the next week, after which I moved out of Craven Terrace and into her studio flat at Kensington Park Gardens. It was not such a reckless and passionate business as it might seem; there was something dream-like in the inevitability of events. We were married at Kensington Register Office. Jo, at twenty-nine, was three years younger than I and I suppose it was quite a late matrimonial start for both of us. We decided to have children as soon as possible.

NOW

SIXTEEN years ago Jo and I were married and now, as Wordsworth's tedious little maid said, we are seven. We have survived, so far. I do not put it more confidently than that because, if I have learnt anything, it is this: that the placing of confidence in the stability of any human relationship is an invitation to providence to slap you down. *On mourra seul*, yes, undeniably we shall, just as each of us lives alone and we can know with certainty as little about another person as we can know of ourselves, and that is very little indeed. The danger in a close human tie like marriage is that intimacy can create the illusion of knowledge, that the husband will deceive himself that he can see into the wife's heart and mind, and the wife will believe that she can predict his reaction to almost any situation because she knows him to the bone when the truth is that no one is knowable in this sense to another. While we are able to startle ourselves we are capable of startling others, and I believe that we, by our nature, are always likely to spring a surprise on ourselves. We must recognize, even in the closest of bonds, that each is alone and each must respect the other's aloneness, the other's mystery, the ability to astonish.

It is late autumn now and Tom Payne's Hill is faint with mist. When I took the dog for a walk yesterday we came back from the village of Trent across the fields just as the afternoon was fading towards evening, and in the milky twilight we could hear the mournful lowing of cattle all about us and I thought this must be just as it was a hundred and more years ago, but for how much longer will it be like this? I wondered if Jacob, my youngest child, would be able in manhood to walk over these fields, feeling something of what I felt then. It seems unlikely and the feeling of probable discontinuity is a little saddening, but reason and instinct tell me that there will always be other comparable experiences through which he, in his own style, will be able to continue and elaborate on my life when I am no longer here to live it myself.

If this sounds morbid and lugubrious it is not a true reflection of my mood. I feel at this moment quite cheerful. I enjoy living in Dorset more and more and, when I have to go away from time to time, I always come back with a sense of relief and pleasure, a confidence in the welcome I am going to receive from the place itself. I have just returned from London where I have been recording for the BBC a longish new poem and also speaking the verse narration of a short radio play. I enjoy these visits but I find that I am still far too easily trapped into drinking too much with old or new friends and spending far more money than I can afford. Now I am at home, hangover subdued, the mind's pencil not too blunt and with about six clear weeks ahead of me with no reviewing, no public readings or other chores, just this book to finish. I shall record the chief personal events of my life until the end of 1960, ten years ago when the pattern for the future seemed to be established, if ever it is and, indeed, if there is such a thing as a pattern for anybody's future. I suspect that these later pages will be more difficult to write because many of the principal events are not yet completed, the situations not resolved. I am still concerned in a very immediate way and unlikely to be able to take the cool and distant view. I shall have to be selective: there are certain people and certain incidents that cannot be mentioned for fear of causing hurt or inviting libel action, but these are few and their omission will not, I think, distort the whole picture, the picture that is of a marriage and of a way of life; a marriage that I would not claim as exemplary but one, as I have said, that has been strong enough to survive sixteen years and a few rough storms which, if not cataclysmic, might still have been turbulent enough to sink a frailer craft.

THEN

SOON after Jo and I were married a friend of hers named Dick Brooman-White, who was a member of Parliament for a Scottish constituency, offered us the tenancy of Pennymore, a farmhouse on the edge of Loch Fyne which he visited only occasionally at weekends and for longer periods when the Commons were in recess. Jo and I were to be unpaid caretakers, but we would live rent-free and when Dick visited he would contribute towards household expenses. We agreed to take it on for six months from October and we thought this period would give me time to write something solid and, we hoped, saleable, a novel or perhaps a play, as well as any poems that came along. Jo's father had given her a hundred pounds as a wedding present and we scraped together another seventy-odd which we reckoned ought to keep us if we lived economically, even if I did not sell any work.

Pennymore was a beautiful old house but it was not very comfortable. There was no electricity and the water supply came from a stream behind the house. Light was provided by oil lamps and we cooked on calor gas. Everything was fine until the really cold weather hit us. Then the stream froze and the water could not get through to our tank so we had to go out and break the ice and draw what we needed in buckets. I was kept fairly busy collecting, sawing and chopping firewood, for we had no other fuel and at night we shivered in a cold and distinctly damp bed.

Jo did some painting and I began to write a novel which I called *Confessions of a Mystified Sinner*, adapting my title from Hogg's wonderful *Justified Sinner*. I sold a couple of poems to English weeklies and one, with Pennymore as its subject, to the *Glasgow Herald*; the fifteen guineas these earned me was all the money I made while we were in Scotland. Jo soon found she was pregnant and for the first couple of months she was appallingly sick, hardly able to digest any food at all. We spent more than we had intended and we were broke long before the six months were over, but we borrowed money and I carried on with the novel, working a good five or six hours a day and finishing the book at the end of February.

Peter Nevill, the publishers of my first two novels, had ceased to exist, and my agent had taken up some other and, I imagine, more lucrative line of business, so I sent my novel directly to an alternative publisher. About a month later it came back with a friendly letter but no offer of publication. I re-parcelled the typescript and sent it out again.

By this time our stay at Pennymore was almost at an end and one morning in early April a letter came from George Scott, who was then the editor of a weekly journal called *Truth*, asking if I would be interested in writing a regular column on sport. *Truth* was a remarkable publication. Its circulation, compared with similar weeklies, was very small and it paid its contributors very poorly, yet it had on its staff a group of young journalists, nearly all of whom were soon to become among the most eminent in their profession. They included Philip Oakes, Bernard Levin and Alan Brien.

I wrote back that I would call on George Scott when I returned to London in a week's time and then we could decide whether the job would suit me and I would suit the job. I had already decided rather nervously that I would accept the offer if it were confirmed though I knew that I was not qualified to write on any other sport than boxing. I had never had more than the most casual interest in team games of any kind, I had taken no part either as competitor or spectator in any kind of athletics since I came fourth in the Sunday School egg-and-spoon race, and I had never held a tennis racquet in my hand. I knew that I would be expected to write about all kinds of sporting activity and doubted my ability to bluff it out but I felt that I could not refuse the offer of a regular income, however small.

Jo was now seven months pregnant, so we borrowed Dick's reasonably comfortable saloon car, drove down to London, where we set up home again in Kensington Park Gardens, and I went to see George Scott and agreed to produce a column the following week. My first piece, predictably enough, was about boxing, a survey of the professional flyweight situation which I called *The Little Men*. My second article was called—I must now admit rather too coyly—*Punch and Judo*, and it was a comparison between the two fighting arts of the East and West, boxing and judo. Before my third contribution was due I decided that I would have to write about something other than combat between two men and here Jo came to the rescue. As a girl, before painting had excluded all other interests, she had been an accomplished horsewoman and that weekend we were visiting her parents at Edenbridge in Kent where the local Hunt was holding its point-to-point.

'Let's go to it,' Jo said. 'You can write a nice atmospheric little piece and I can give you a bit of the jargon and so on.'

The collaboration proved acceptable to the editor so I looked around for other knowledgeable people to help me out. Jo's father, who was an ex-rugger player, produced a highly technical analysis of the faults and merits of the English and French sides who were shortly to meet at Twickenham, Jo covered a hockey international and a cricketing friend supplied me with a prophetic survey of the coming season which was not difficult to paraphrase. I began to develop a slick style and a way of hinting at sporting information, which I alone possessed, without actually divulging it. As I grew more experienced I covered a wider range of games including rowing, soccer, tennis, croquet at Roehampton, water polo at Lime Grove Baths and the Eton and Harrow match at Lords. I even wrote an account of a pub darts match one week when I was pressed for time and material. If I learnt anything from my stint as a sporting journalist it was to view all experts with suspicion.

I was still not earning enough to keep us, so I vigilantly watched the Vacancies columns of the dailies and weeklies. Then in the *New Statesman* I saw an advertisement asking for a writer and lecturer to undertake propaganda work for 'an animal protection society'. I wrote a letter of application and a reply came back from The National Anti-Vivisection Society asking me to attend for an interview at their offices in Victoria Street, where I spent a mildly embarrassing half-hour with the Secretary, a tiny, stooped, Dickensian old man with a bald head that looked as if it was covered with parchment.

He said, 'We would want you to look after our monthly Bulletin which is sent out to all our members. That means you have to keep an eye on the press and on the medical and scientific publications for any details of animal experimentation, and you make the gruesome business public in the Bulletin. I am sure we can rely on your pen. But there's another side to the duties you would be expected to perform. You'd be called on to give lectures on our cause to schools, societies and so on whenever they were required.'

I said that I could hardly be asked to lecture on something I knew nothing about.

'You know nothing at all about our work here?'

'I'm afraid not.'

'Ah, I will supply you with literature before you go. I will give you C. S. Lewis's pamphlet which he has written especially for the Society. I don't think you will be able to deny that our cause is just.'

I wanted the job, any job, so I nodded, showing my readiness to be converted.

'The point is,' the Secretary said, 'will you be any good at public speaking?'

'I've done a bit of broadcasting and I used to teach. I ought to be all right.'

'Yes, but we have to be sure. Now, would you mind giving me a little sample lecture. Just to show how your platform manner would be. Any subject you like, anything that you can talk for ten minutes or so about.'

'Now?'

'Yes, that's what I said. Now.' He spoke testily like a schoolmaster losing patience with a slow-witted boy.

The situation began to seem unreal. I sat opposite the old man in his dusty office with the large desk between us and huge brown portraits of prominent Victorian anti-vivisectionists on the walls. I wondered if I was supposed to stand up and adopt an oratorial pose.

'Go on,' he said.

I could think of nothing to say. Then I remembered my last broadcast talk, which had been about Englishmen in Scottish regiments during the last war, and I began to speak, partly from memory of the script and improvising when necessary.

Presently he said, 'That'll do. Yes, thank you. That seems to be all right. There shouldn't be any difficulty there. Now I'll give you some things to take home and read and we'll be writing to you to confirm your appointment. I think you can take it that we will pleased to have you with us.'

We shook hands and I left the office and caught a fifty-two bus back to Notting Hill Gate.

Jo and I read the pamphlets and books that I had brought back with me and we were both more impressed than we had expected to be by the strength of the case for anti-vivisection. It seemed beyond question that the controls over animal experimentation and the way that inspections were carried out were totally inadequate and a great deal of suffering was inflicted on living creatures without reasonable justification. The Secretary had shown some perception in giving me the C. S. Lewis pamphlet because this was a closely reasoned argument, lacking the hysterical indignation of some of the other propaganda, questioning the moral right of men to subject weaker animals to great pain in the hope that some of their own sufferings might be mitigated. If we accept the notion that man is entitled to use lower creatures as he pleases, to induce cancerous growths, for example, in the bodies of rats or apes, how can we object if he decides, as the Nazis decided, that certain kinds of humans are so low in the scale of things that it is legitimate to use them in the same way. The principles of vivisection led to the human experiments performed in the concentration camps. What I found a lot less persuasive about much of the literature was something which I have often noticed among people with an exaggerated love of animals, that is a corresponding distaste for humans, but I thought that I would be able to work for the cause without serious compromise of principle.

A couple of days later the Secretary wrote offering me the job at a salary of five hundred pounds a year, so apart from my weekly column for *Truth* I had to produce a monthly news-sheet for the Society, swot up on the history of the movement and study the various polemics defending the cause. Then, every two weeks or so, I had to drive off in the Society's little Ford van, which was plastered with horrifying pictures of tortured animals, to different parts of England to lecture or rather preach a gospel to which I was less than totally committed. I was earning just about enough to keep us, but I was miserably aware that I had no hope of ever having time to write what I wanted to. My novel came back from a third and then a fourth publisher and I began to think they were probably right in rejecting it. When it came back from a fifth consideration, I read a few pages, decided it was rubbish, and chucked it into a corner in disgust. It must have gone into the dustbin later on because I have no recollection of it after that day.

Then something happened that jolted me out of my gloom. I came home from the office in the early evening to find Jo in a state of alarm and excitement.

'I think it's started!' she said. 'I think the baby's coming.'

I got her into a taxi and took her to St George's Hospital at Hyde Park Corner where she was to have the child. When Jo had been taken away by a nurse the ward Sister told me that it would probably be a long time before the baby arrived and my best plan was to go away and ring up later on or the next morning when they would almost certainly have news for me.

I left the hospital and walked back through the park and went to The Chepstow for a drink. Time passed very slowly. At nine I telephoned the hospital and was told to ring the next morning. I tried again at ten o'clock and was told the same thing. I carried on drinking and went to bed that night fairly sodden but I was awake soon after six o'clock and when I rang St George's I was told that Jo had given birth in the early hours of the morning to a daughter. All I felt was relief that she had come through the ordeal safely. No sudden paternal tenderness was aroused. I wanted to see Jo but I did not feel much, beyond a mild curiosity, about the baby who was to be called Jane; it was not until Jo brought her home from the hospital that the change occurred, but when it came it was overwhelming.

The first indication of the fact that the birth of Jane had altered me was when I found myself peering into parked perambulators outside shops and eyeing the occupants with great interest, often causing grave alarm to mothers who imagined their babies were being threatened by a maniac. Then I discovered that I was hurrying straight home from work, untempted by the open doors of the public houses, impatient to see my daughter, and I suddenly realized that this tiny person had altered me, fundamentally and irrevocably, that her advent had created inside me areas of feeling that had not previously existed, that for the first time in my life I was capable of experiencing something approaching selfless love. I was deeply and humbly grateful for the change.

Jo was amused. Before her daughter was born she had listened to me speaking of babies as little vegetables. I had predicted that I would be able to take little interest in the child until it was old enough to walk and talk, to be a companion. For the first year or so all babies were alike: they made unpleasant noises and smells. The man who pretended enjoyment in such company must be a hypocrite. Now she watched me with a grin, relishing my delight and terror, terror because of my child's appalling frailty, the nameless menaces that were marshalling to threaten her safety.

Jo said, 'This is an interesting case. Fixated on a vegetable. Very strange.'

Jane had enriched my life but I was finding my work growing steadily more onerous and there were times when I felt that I was trapped. I continued to write the weekly column for *Truth* and I gave frequent lectures on the evils of animal vivisection to bored schoolchildren, mad vegetarian societies and sceptical audiences from youth clubs. I also began to despair of ever having the leisure and energy to write the poems I believed were waiting to be hammered out. Then a difficulty arose about the renewal of the lease for the flat and it seemed as if we would have to look for somewhere else to live. I had a silly row with the Secretary at the Society over my travelling expenses and I was feeling victimized, depressed and frustrated. The beautiful summer weather seemed to mock my grey mood. I knew suddenly that I had to escape from the sterile and meaningless routine that I had allowed to imprison me.

I said to Jo, 'How do you feel about trying to get out of London?'

She did not hesitate. 'I think it would be marvellous. I've never liked the idea of bringing up a family in a town. But where could we go and what would we live on? I can't see you as a cowman.'

I thought for a while and then said that the only job I might be able to find in the country would be teaching.

'That might be the answer,' Jo said. 'There's a prep school near home in Kent. My father's quite friendly with the Headmaster.'

Her brother, Patrick, had been taught there, the Headmaster, who owned the school, was well-disposed to the whole family and Jo felt that this good feeling might be extended to me. 'We'll go down this weekend. I'll get my father to fix a meeting. I know they used to change half their staff every term. If things are the same as when Patrick was there they might have a job for you next term.'

It turned out to be wonderfully simple. Although the month was August and the boys, of course, were on holiday, the Headmaster was at home and he invited me to call on him on the Sunday afternoon when, after a quarter of an hour's chat and a large whisky each, it was decided that I would start at the beginning of the Michaelmas term teaching English throughout the school at a salary of five hundred a year. He gave me the address of the man whose place I would be taking, a South African who was returning to his native country, and said that in all probability I would be able to rent the cottage that the previous English master was vacating. So I went into the village and found the house, a tiny crumbling place that was supposed to date back to the fourteenth century. The South African was sure that there would be no difficulty in my taking over the tenancy from him and, if all went well, I would be able to move in at the beginning of September.

Jo and I and the baby returned to London and on Monday morning I handed in my notice at the Society, but I decided that, for the time being, I would hang on to the *Truth* column in the hope that I would be able to get my weekly piece written from the country. So, in September 1955, we left Kensington Park Gardens and settled in the little cottage. Once again I found myself engaged in teaching the young.

*

The village, though within easy reach of London and with a high percentage of its inhabitants commuting to the City, managed to retain much of its original rural nature because the place itself and a good deal of the surrounding countryside came under the protection of the National Trust, and the businesses of the shopkeepers and tradesmen, the greengrocer, the butcher and the baker whose wife was the postmistress, the plumber and the undertaker, were all in the hands of families who had lived in the place for generations. There were two pubs and in both of these one heard the slow local speech of farm-workers mixed with the standard, ex-public school voices of stock-brokers, insurance underwriters and high-powered sales-managers.

The school where I taught was about a mile's walk from the cottage. The main building was a Victorian mansion with generous grounds, a swimming pool, tennis court and croquet lawn as well as rugger pitches and a small but carefully tended cricket ground. Beyond the cricket field, there were two smaller houses where the older boys slept, while the younger ones had their dormitories in the school itself, close to the Matron and the Headmaster's wife.

It was not a bad school as such places go and though discipline was strict and the teaching dull on the whole and, at times, grossly incompetent, the boys seemed to enjoy themselves, and the Victorian orthodoxy of the curriculum was to some extent offset by the individual peculiarities and attitudes of some of the more eccentric masters. We were paid badly and expected to do a lot for a little. The working day began with chapel at a quarter to nine in the morning followed by five teaching periods with a break at eleven and lunch at one. After lunch the whole school played compulsory games which were supervised by the masters, many of whom were not only ignorant of the rules of the particular sport they were supposed to be coaching but vociferously and bitterly hated all forms of outdoor games. There were two more lessons after games at four o'clock; tea, which was the boys' last meal of the day, was at five-thirty and then there was a session of evening prep to be supervised by the duty-master. On Sundays there were two masters who had to be on duty from breakfast until bedtime, taking the boys for long walks in the afternoon and reading to them in the evening before seeing them tucked in for the night.

At first I found it all rather fascinating. It was a world I had heard of but never before entered, and the rites, the values, the superstitions, the language itself, were all strange to me. I do not think there can be many such schools left today. Physical toughness and courage were the attributes most highly prized by the Head and, officially and often hypocritically, by the boys and staff; most punishments were corporal, beatings or immensely long cross-country runs before breakfast. The most common and despicable crime was 'slackness' which could mean poor performance in class or on the sports field irrespective of aptitude; untidiness, un-punctuality, the loss of possessions or, least forgivable of all, bed-wetting. Bullying, unless it was flagrant, was largely ignored and even condoned as possessing educative value for the victim who must learn to face injustice, adversity and bodily pain with fortitude and without complaint. Sneaking was rare because those who had tried it had found that it brought only universal contempt and no redress of the wrong complained about.

The school was divided into Houses, each one named after an Old Boy who had distinguished himself for gallantry in the First World War, and the rivalry between them was intense. At the end of every term the whole school assembled for a ceremony called 'mark-reading' when each boy was individually dealt with, commanded to stand up, blushing with shame or pride, as the Headmaster read aloud the marks he had gained throughout the term for 'work', 'games', 'effort', and 'character'. This last mark, for 'character', was reached at an end-of-term staff meeting when each boy was discussed by all the masters, under the chairmanship of the Head, and each of us was required to award a mark out of ten. Conspicuously spineless boys could be stigmatized with a minus mark. I remember one of these occasions when a rather unpopular boy came up for discussion, and one of my colleagues, a choleric and sublimely stupid ex-Army officer, said, 'That's boy's a coward. I'd give him a minus.'

One of the other masters protested. 'Oh, I wouldn't say that at all. He's done some jolly good tackling on the rugger field and he's held his own in any fight he's been in as far as I know.'

'Perhaps so,' said the gallant officer, 'but would he face cold steel?'

I have often seen little boys at 'mark-reading' weeping from remorse and shame at having let down the House.

There was something dreamlike about much of school life, moments of Alice-in-Wonderland craziness, an unnerving sense of lunacy in command, together with a vague sense of *déjà vu* which I think must have come from residual memories of my reading the *Magnet* and *The Gem* when I was about the same age as the boys I was teaching. But after my first few weeks I began to find the place oppressive. What had before seemed comical or quaint started to irritate and, though some of the boys were very bright and seemed to enjoy both reading and writing poems and stories, the syllabus, geared as it was to the antiquated Public Schools Common Entrance Examination, discouraged originality from either teacher or pupil. Apart from one or two eccentrics, the masters were drab at best and imbecilic at worst, and the fact that they were there because they were unemployable anywhere else was not reassuring. After all, I was one of them, too.

At home, money was a nagging worry that rarely let us alone and, at the end of my second term, Jo became pregnant again. I had lost my job with *Truth* because it was impossible for me to get away from the village to cover any important sporting function, so after writing two or three generalized pieces I found myself, a single day from the deadline, with nothing at all to write about. Then I remembered that a 'conkers' craze was raging at the school, so I wrote an account of a David and Goliath encounter between a tiny conker and a gigantic one which was smashed to fragments by the midget. In the past I had got away with a good deal but this was too much for George Scott and I had to agree with him that the time had come for me to surrender my column to someone who would produce more orthodox sporting journalism.

Once more, in my search for a way of life that would allow me time and energy for what I regarded as my real job of writing poetry, I had saddled myself with employment that was too exacting during term-time and so badly paid that, in the holidays, I had to spend my time trying to earn money. I did write a few poems but I wasted innumerable working hours in struggling to produce short stories, which I hoped might prove remunerative (though they never were), and I did some private coaching which was certain at least to bring in some money, however little. But towards the end of 1956 my prospects began to look a bit brighter.

A little press, Villiers Publications, was bringing out a collection of my poems which I called *A Mortal Pitch*, and an anthology with the title *Mavericks*, intended to represent poets who had not been included in Robert Conquest's *New Lines* (the 'Movement' anthology), was being prepared by Howard Sergeant and Dannie Abse who used five poems of mine. I was writing more regularly and working hard at poems and I hoped I could see the beginnings of an individual tone emerging. Then, on December 4, my second daughter, Nancy, was born and I knew that, now we were a family of four, I had to look for a bigger home.

There was an empty house on the village High Street, a neat Queen Anne double-fronted cottage, and I had peered into the front rooms and seen built-in bookshelves along the walls.

I said to Jo, 'That place would suit us. It's got three bedrooms and quite a good-sized garden. I wonder who owns it.'

We made enquiries and found out from the agent who represented the owner that it was for sale at the surprisingly low sum, in such an expensive area, of a little over three thousand pounds. As far as we were concerned, I thought, it might just as well be three million. But I was wrong. Jo's mother, who was concerned for her daughter's health and happiness in the tiny and inconvenient cottage we were living in, volunteered to draw out some of her capital to buy the house and we could pay her in rent whatever interest she would be losing. This arrangement could not have been better from my point of view, for the rent would be less than what I was already handing out for the place we were in.

The negotiations with agents and solicitors and then having builders in to do some necessary repairs took quite a long time but, since we knew we were going to move, we were much happier in the little cottage and were able to contain our impatience. It was quite early in 1958, about April or May, that we moved into the house. Now I found it much easier to work since I could use the sitting-room as a study, and gradually my fortunes improved. I was writing fairly steadily, publishing poems in the weeklies and doing a few broadcasts on George MacBeth's Third Programme arts review, *Comment*. Corgi Books brought out a paperback edition of my first novel, *The Fight*, which earned a little extra money, and I began to write a thriller, not at the expense of the poetry but working on it only when I felt I had nothing more worthwhile to do. And, as if I had not enough on my hands, I took on a weekly evening class in the nearest town, conducting a course on Creative Writing. By the end of the year I had finished the thriller, it had been accepted by John Long, a subsidiary of Hutchinson specializing in crime fiction, and I was putting together another collection of poems.

With two children under the age of four, Jo had no time for painting but she did not complain and I think she was finding the plunge into domesticity a useful and guiltless way of shelving the many theoretical and practical problems which had been harassing her immediately before we married. Untrained and not temperamentally fitted to the housewife's role, she was spending far more nervous and physical energy than the natural *Hausfrau* would believe possible. As the summer term of 1959 drew to a close, I decided that we both needed a holiday, however brief, and I suggested that we should leave Jane and Nancy with her mother and go off to Paris for a lazy week on our own.

'And what would we use for money?' Jo reasonably asked.

We were managing to keep solvent, but only just.

I said, 'I'll write something quickly. If it comes off we'll go.'

'What sort of thing are you going to write?'

'Another thriller.'

For some weeks an idea for a psychological thriller had been lurking around the borders of my imagination, at times moving into the centre, and I knew that I would have to get rid of it sooner or later by trapping it in language. So, as soon as school broke up, I sat down at my desk and rapidly sketched out the plot of the tale. Then I went to work, composing straight on to the typewriter, tapping away from morning to night and, at the end of three weeks, the book was finished and ready to be sent off to the publishers. I gave it the title of *The Shadowed Place* and gave Jo the typescript to read.

She said, 'It's fine. I was quite frightened.'

'Then let's take a chance,' I said. 'I'll send it to John Long and rely on their taking it. They'll pay an advance of seventy-five pounds so let's allow ourselves fifty and go. If they turn it down I'll probably be able to find another publisher for it and if I can't we won't starve.'

So we left the children with their grandparents and went to Paris for a week of modest self-indulgence. The weather was fine and we enjoyed wandering about the streets, looking at pictures, eating and drinking well but not extravagantly. When we returned I found among the waiting mail a letter from the publishers, Putnam, saying that they would be pleased to bring out my new book of poems, *The Masks of Love*, and one from John Long accepting *The Shadowed Place*. Jo found that she was pregnant again.

*

Nineteen hundred and sixty was, in many ways, a fateful year for us. From the point of view of my work, it saw me setting out on the path towards freedom from the necessity to teach or to take on any other kind of full-time job, and heading towards a position where I would be able to earn enough to keep us on what I was paid for my writing and ancillary activities such as broadcasting, reviewing, lecturing and the poetry-readings which were just beginning to become popular and remunerative. At the beginning of the year *The Masks of Love* was published and I started to write a novel, *The Face of the Enemy*, which was completed and accepted for publication by the end of August; John Long also sold the Norwegian serial rights of my first thriller. More invitations to give public readings of my poems were coming in, and it was on one of these occasions that I met for the first time Robert Gittings, who was then working for BBC Radio as a producer in the Schools Department.

We were chatting over a drink when Robert said, 'I've read your novel about boxing. How do you feel about writing a narrative poem about the game? What I have in mind is a direct piece of writing which ought to appeal to a young audience. If you decide you'd like to have a shot I'll arrange for you to be commissioned, half the fee on signature of contract and the other half when you've delivered the goods.'

The idea appealed to me and a few weeks later I had finished a poem called *First Fight* which described a young boxer taking part in his first professional contest, showing him in the dressing-room, stretched on a rack of nervous excitement and foreboding, his entering the ring, and then an account of the fight itself with a short closing section showing the boy, lying in bed at home after he has won the bout, when he thinks with pity and a touch of remorse of his opponent, someone who, like himself, had gone into the ring full of ambition, hope and fear, and must now surely be sick with the taste of defeat and failure. Then the young boxer realizes that 'Fighters can't pack pity with their gear', that everyone's success is contingent on another's failure, that there can be no victor unless there is also the vanquished.

The poem was broadcast and, although I have not included it in any of my published collections, it has appeared in quite a few anthologies and was subsequently re-broadcast and has earned me over the years a fair amount of money. But what was more important at the time was that it showed to me that I could not only write on a theme suggested by someone else, but that I actually found the external pressures, the challenge of producing something that would not disappoint the sponsor and meeting a firm deadline, creatively stimulating. In fact, the whole of that period was exuberantly productive and I look back with a kind of incredulous envy at my industry of ten years ago: apart from completing my novel I wrote a lot of the poems that were to appear in my next collection, *A Sense of Danger*, I did a fair amount of broadcasting and reviewing and I was still teaching full-time, lecturing one evening a week and doing some private coaching. I also took on the job, with Ted Hughes and Patricia Beer, of editing the next anthology of the P.E.N. Club.

When I said that 1960 was a fateful time I did not mean only that it was decisive for my future as a writer; an event occurred in that year that still haunts me and will continue to haunt me to the end of my days. Jo, you may remember, was pregnant on our return from the short holiday in Paris, and, as she grew monstrously big, her doctor began to wonder how many babies she was carrying. Manipulation suggested that there were twins and an X-ray confirmed their presence.

After the initial mild hysteria that the knowledge caused, we quickly grew accustomed to the prospect of having two more children instead of one, and we started to prepare ourselves by acquiring, second-hand, a twin pram and an extra cot and deciding on two girls' names and two boys' so that we would be armed whatever sex or mixture of sexes the twins turned out to be.

The winter gave way to spring and Jo grew closer to the time of her confinement which was to take place in Redhill Hospital. On the day that the ambulance carried her away I took Jane and Nancy over to their grandparents at Edenbridge where we were all staying for a few days and, early the next morning, I telephoned the hospital.

I held the receiver to my ear and heard the mechanical jets of noise in the darkness, the quick double rasps, repeated four or five times. Then a voice said, 'Redhill Hospital. Can I help you?'

I asked for the maternity ward.

A few moments later another woman's voice came on to the line. I told her who I was and asked for news of Jo and the twins. She seemed to hesitate for a fraction of a second before she answered and I felt, even then, a cold tremor of uncertainty, a blind premonition of misfortune.

She said, 'Mrs Scannell has given birth to twin boys.' Again that slight hesitation. 'The first baby is perfectly healthy but I'm afraid that the other . . . is not quite . . .' she hurried on: '. . . we think the best thing would be for you to come and see the doctor. He'll explain everything.'

I said, 'You mean he's deformed?'

'I'm sorry, Mr Scannell, I can't really give you any details. I simply don't know anything except that one baby is not as well as he should be. You come to the hospital and speak to the doctor. He'll tell you everything.'

'When can I come?'

'Could you be here at ten o'clock this morning?'

I said that I could and I rang off. I felt dazed and sickened, very much as if I had taken a heavy punch under the heart. Jo's mother was hovering anxiously and I realized that she must have heard me use the word 'deformed'. I told her the little I knew and she, too, looked stunned and wretched and I thought—though this may only have been my own feeling of irrational guilt—a little accusing.

I tried to reassure her. 'It might not be too bad. The woman didn't seem to know much about it.'

She nodded, but she was not listening, and I thought, not for the first time, that women always take the heaviest punishment. She set about preparing breakfast for Jane and Nancy and I went up to my room and smoked until my mouth was parched and bitter. I tried not to keep looking at my watch. I went out into the garden where the apple trees were in blossom and the birds were jubilant in the morning sun. I tried not to think about the deformed baby but I could not prevent the images from invading the mind, images spawned by scraps of gossip, half-remembered and probably untrue in the first place, of human monsters, alive but hidden from public view in special hospitals and asylums, obscenities with the heads of rodents on scaly bodies, huge cyclopic heads on tiny trunks, malformations of hands and feet, a faceless head, a living bladder of lard with orifices only for breathing and eating. When I tried to tell myself that I was almost certainly exaggerating the affliction of my baby, that he was most likely only suffering from some minor disfiguration or handicap, I found that my mind swung away from more comfortable speculation to welcome back the nightmare images, because it dared not face the possibility that the reality might be worse than the imagined condition.

At half-past nine I borrowed my father-in-law's car and drove to the hospital. I was a little early but the doctor saw me straight away. He was a dark, tired-looking man, mercifully unfussy and practical.

He said, 'I am afraid this is a very unpleasant shock for you. As you know, one of the babies seems to be perfectly normal. A normal delivery, quite an easy one. The second wasn't so easy. He's suffering from what is called a meningocele, that's a hernia of the meninges, the membranes over the brain and spinal cord. He's got a big swelling on the back of his head and this will have to be removed. I think the chances of his surviving this are pretty good but how much brain damage he's likely to suffer I couldn't possibly say. I'm not a specialist on this, you see. But I know enough about it to say that the damage might be very considerable indeed. Encephalitis is common with these cases and you can be certain that the child will never be able to lead a normal life. I'd go as far as to say that it's very doubtful that he'd be able to walk or talk, though—

189

as I've said—you must wait for specialist opinion before you decide what you're going to do.'

I must have looked blank. 'Do?'

He said, 'I mean whether you would look after the child yourselves or leave him in the hospital he'd be sent to for the operation. That's St Mary's at Carshalton. They look after a lot of similar cases there.'

I said, 'I see.' But I did not see or feel much at all. A sense of unreality was settling over me, cushioning me against the sharper edges of what was happening.

'What about Jo?' I said. 'My wife. Does she know about this?'

'She's been told only that the second twin is weak and has a spinal injury. We thought it might be better if you told her the facts.'

'Yes, I suppose so.'

He said, 'Would you like to see the baby? I must warn you that he's not—that the growth is large and unsightly. You might prefer not to . . . for the present, anyway . . .'

'Yes, I'd like to see him.'

I was not so sure that I did want to see him, but I felt I could not tell Jo about his condition unless I knew what he looked like.

'Very well.'

I followed the doctor along some corridors and we stopped outside a door.

'You sure you wouldn't like to leave it till a bit later?' he said.

I felt a flutter at the heart, a blurring of vision and a weakness in the legs. Panic. Was the baby so hideous? Would I make a fool of myself, be sick on the spot or collapse in a dead faint?'

'No. I want to see him now.' I was mildly surprised that my voice sounded quite calm and firm.

We went into the room. There were a dozen or so incubators in it, each one like a glass box with a doll inside.

The doctor said, 'Here we are, this is the one.'

I realized that my fists were tightly clenched and I was digging the fingernails into the palms of my hands. I looked and, for a second, I was utterly bewildered and, wildly, I wondered if I could be the victim of a lunatic hoax. Then I felt a surge of relief that was instantly followed by a drench of pure joy and wonder at the beauty of the child. I had never seen anything so beautiful. He lay on one side with his eyes closed, and the tiny features looked at once exquisitely carved yet tenderly human like the head of one of those babies you see in fifteenth-century Flemish paintings, an idealization of the infant. I could see one tiny hand, perfectly formed, the minute fingers curved near his cheek. The swelling at the back of the head seemed irrelevant; it ballooned out, a dark congested purple, a little like the bulb on an old fashioned motor horn, about the size of the head itself. It could have been something left there by mistake, touching the little skull but not really connected to it. I looked closer and saw that the meningocele was indeed a malignant appendage attached to the back of the little head but I could feel no horror, only wonder that a child so handicapped could be so beautiful.

The doctor said, 'All right, Mr Scannell?'

I said, 'He's marvellous.'

I felt his hand on my arm. I think he was afraid that I might behave in some unpredictable and embarrassing manner.

I said, 'All right, thank you,' and he took me out of the room and directed me to the ward where Jo lay, a cot beside her bed with the other twin in it.

She was awake and she looked pale but quite composed.

She said, 'Have you seen Benjamin?'

I nodded. 'That's his name, is it?'

'Yes. He's been baptized already. They said he was weak. They baptize them at once if they think . . . have you seen him? Yes, you just said you had. What's he like? Is he all right?'

'He's fine. He's beautiful. But there's something wrong with him. He's going to be okay, I think. I mean he's going to survive. But he'll be handicapped.' I knew that she would not wish me to tell her anything but the truth as I knew it so I repeated to her all that the doctor had told me.

I held her hand. 'Don't worry,' I said. 'Everything's going to be all right. He's going to be fine. Believe me. He's the nicest baby I've ever seen.'

I thought she was going to cry but she did not. She said, 'We'll keep him at home, won't we? Whatever he's like? Whatever happens?'

'Of course.'

'Good. I thought you'd say that.'

We sat for a while, not saying much. Then Jo said, 'You haven't looked at Toby.'

'Toby?'

'Tobias. Your other son.'

I looked into the cot at the bedside. It contained a baby, an ordinary baby.

Jo said, 'Isn't he lovely?'

'Yes, he's lovely.'

But all I could think of was the tiny creature in the glass box, his grave sleeping face, the little head resting against the swollen bulb of dark flesh.

Presently a nurse came along and told me that I must leave. I said goodbye to Jo and promised to return that evening. I went out of the hospital. Outside, the sun was still shining and the air was sweet after the hospital smell. I got into the car and drove back to Edenbridge.

*

We brought Benjamin home from Carshalton towards the end of May. The woman specialist I had spoken to at St Mary's gave us cautious encouragement but was careful not to raise false hopes.

'It is impossible to predict what progress he may make,' she had said. 'But you must realize that he will never be a normal human being. There is absolutely no question of that. At the same time, there's no doubt that a child like this responds far better to the love and care of parents and brothers and sisters in its own home than ever he could to the necessarily more impersonal attention he would get here.'

At nights it was my responsibility to feed Benjamin while Jo was attending to Toby's needs. Benjamin was very frail and, on the rare occasions when he cried, his voice was paper-thin, fluttering on silence like the wings of a dying moth. I still found his face beautiful though I had to admit that it showed none of the expression that

Toby's was beginning to display. He would lie, almost weightlessly, in the crook of my arm, so small and so fragile that it seemed impossible that he could be a living human, and after he had taken the little nourishment that he could swallow, I would very softly pat and massage his back until he expelled a tiny gust of wind. I would nurse him for a while, looking into his face for some sign of animation, but it always remained quite expressionless, the eyes either closed or apparently unseeing, a small breathing statue. There was a little lump on the back of his head where the meningocele had been removed. Otherwise, apart from his smallness and impassivity, he looked like any baby except that, to me, his minuscule features were more delicately shaped than any I had seen or could imagine.

Jo and I found ourselves coming to terms with the prospect of living with a severely handicapped member of the family, and we were both surprised at the equanimity with which we could envisage the future. I suddenly remembered a family I had known during the war when I was in the convalescent depot at Hamilton. The father was a miner and both of his bachelor sons had followed him into the pits. Neither of his daughters was married, and one of them, Mary, never would be, for she was unable to stand and she could slur out only a few recognizable words. She was about nineteen or twenty but she crawled about the floor, drooling and chuckling like an enormous baby.

When I had first been invited to the home I had found myself physically repelled by Mary, but this feeling had quickly disappeared when I had seen how everyone in the family unaffectedly loved her and delighted in her existence. Soon I came to understand that these people, far from being burdened or diminished by the presence among them of the badly handicapped girl, considered themselves blessed and enriched, and indeed they all—the hardbitten father and ribald sons, the harassed yet always genial mother, and the other daughter, Rae, vivacious and pretty—seemed finer, more sympathetic, tolerant and alive than most other families in whatever material circumstances.

I told Jo about Mary. I said, 'One thing was sure. Whatever anguish they might have gone through when the child was born, or when they first realized what was wrong with her, and whatever anguish the future held for them, there was not a shadow of doubt that they were mighty grateful that they'd got her.'

Jo and I did not, I am sure, hide from the realities of the situation. We both knew that Benjamin, as he grew older, would become a restraint on our freedom. We both faced the fact that he might never even reach the stage of development that Mary attained, might never perhaps recognize or be able to communicate with us at all, and, as we sternly reminded each other, he would not remain a baby for long; he would grow big and, perhaps, monstrous. It did not matter. We would have to face the fresh problems as they arose. Here and now we were grateful for Benjamin; we, too, felt blessed.

We watched his progress with microscopic care, worrying when he would not take his milk, rejoicing when he seemed hungry, and at nights, however deep our sleep, we would be instantly awakened by his wispy cries. We noticed that there were times when he seemed to find difficulty in breathing and you could hear the faint rasping in the frail cage of his chest and the rate of his breathing seemed too fast. When we took him to our doctor we were told that there was some bronchial congestion but it would probably clear itself up.

One night in late August, or rather in the early hours of the morning, after I had fed Benjamin and seen him back into his cot, I was slipping back into sleep when I was jerked awake by a faint noise. I sat up and listened. Again I heard the sound; it was not his usual dry fluttering cry, but a noise I had never before heard him make, a brief and very soft chirrup and twitter like birds settling in their nests for the night but heard from a considerable distance. I slipped out of bed and went to his side. A night light burned on the chest-of-drawers and shadows made obeisances on the walls. I looked down and saw that Benjamin's eyes were not closed. I bent close and he seemed to be looking back at me.

I waited to see if he would make the sound again but all I could hear was the slight wheezing of his rapid breathing. The little head looked unbearably vulnerable. His eyes were still open. I wished that he would make his new sound again but he just lay there and seemed to return my scrutiny with incurious serenity. Then, just as I was about to go back to bed, the miracle occurred. Benjamin smiled. For the first time the small, almost mask-like face was illumined from within and it became, instead of an idealization or caricature of infancy, wonderfully and unequivocally human, and the opening of the lips, the upwards curve of each corner of the mouth and the narrowing of eyes, disturbing the perfection of the features in repose, thrilled me with their sweet and mortal imperfection. The smile lasted for perhaps two or three seconds. Then his eyes closed, the little mask of gravity was resumed, and he slept. I have since been told that all I saw was a trick of the flickering candlelight playing over his face or a spasm of indigestion contorting his features, but I am not convinced. I am sure that he smiled.

The next afternoon I had to go to London to see Roger Lubbock, the Chairman of Putnams, about my novel, *The Face of the Enemy*. He had one or two points to make about the last chapter, which we discussed, finally arranging that I should make some small modifications. After I left the office I went to a small drinking club near Broadcasting House where I met John Davenport and other friends for a convivial couple of hours. I stayed longer than I had intended and I had to hurry to catch the 7.10 from Victoria. It was a fine evening. I walked the mile or so from the station to the village and I reached home soon after eight o'clock. I went into the house and found no one downstairs. I looked in the garden but Jo was not there so I started to go upstairs just as she appeared from our bedroom. I waited for her to come down.

I saw immediately that something was wrong. She looked pale; her eyes had a fixed brightness and her mouth was hard and twisted as if she were biting on something that tasted very bitter.

My heart began to thump with a sudden alarm. I said, 'What's the matter?'

She shook her head with a single flick as if deflecting the question I had thrown at her.

I let her pass me and then I followed her into the kitchen at the back of the house. She sat down at the table. Then her mouth went loose, her face twisted as if she had felt a quick thrust of pain and tears began to stream down her cheeks.

She said, 'Benjamin's dead.'

I sat down. I could taste beer, sour and rebellious in the stomach and throat. I felt parched and sick and I began to tremble.

I said, 'Benjamin?' as if I could not believe what she had said, but it seemed that I had known before she had spoken.

Jo began to speak very quickly and all the time the tears were streaming down her face. 'It wasn't my fault. It was about two o'clock. He started to breathe fast and he couldn't—he didn't seem able to get enough air. Then his face went blue. He couldn't breathe. I picked him up and put him in the car and drove as fast as I could to the hospital. They took him away and I waited. I waited. It wasn't my fault. They said there was nothing I could have done. He just died.'

I sat opposite Jo and watched her cry. I knew I ought to do something to comfort her but I did nothing. I saw that each of us was alone now. There was nothing, for the moment, that we could do to help one another. Later, perhaps, but not now. I got up and went into the garden. I thought, 'He's gone. There wasn't much of him and now there's nothing.' I did not feel angry—not then—but there was a wedge of pain, dry and abrasive, like a growth in my throat. I thought if I could cry it might help. It might flush the quinsy of grief. But I could not cry. I had not cried for longer than I could remember and, in any case, it would be absurd for a man of my age to be standing in his garden on a summer evening bawling his eyes out. Grown men did not cry. They knew it served no purpose. It was something that women and children did, something you outgrew; its impossibility defined the adult male. It might have helped, though, had it been possible. It might, if only for the moment, ease the immediate pain. Then I noticed the hot prickle and itch on my face and I found that I had been crying all the time, but it did not help very much. The pain of loss was not to be washed away by a few drops of salty water. I would have to get accustomed to it; it would become familiar and therefore bearable, but it would stay with me for ever.

NOW

IT IS Boxing Day and the fresh snow covers Tom Payne's Hill and ermines the branches of the tree outside my window. The children have enjoyed their Christmas but now they are suffering the inevitable anti-climax: the glitter has dimmed, the wonderful present has lost its newness yet has not had time to become known and friendly. John, aged nine, is jealous of Jacob who, at three, is the youngest, and he devises subtle forms of mild torment for his little brother; Toby says he is bored and Jane and Nancy bicker irritably. Jo is at the ironing-board and I lurk in my room and chew an indigestion tablet while I read *The Dunciad* and wait for The Griffin's Head to open.

Yesterday I read through this book and tried to see if there was any pattern, any instructive logic of events on which I might plan the future, and I have found in this random narrative of experience and occurrences something that I suppose ought not to surprise me; and it is this: under all the confusion, waste and perplexity of living, there has been a steady purpose, that, though I have often appeared to be, and believed myself to be, lost and blundering around in circles, I have in fact been moving fairly consistently in a particular direction, towards the fulfilment of my ambition to be a poet. I am not making claims for myself or for the poetry that I have written. I well believe that there are many readers who would say: 'He's no more likely to fulfil that ambition than he is to live to a thousand', and I admit that they may be perfectly right. It is beside the point, which is that I have lived, and will continue to live, as if the possibility were real; and in doing so I have been rewarded with a sense of direction that I would otherwise lack and without which I would be truly lost.